LOVE, SEX,
AND
MAGICK

Other books by Sirona Knight

Celtic Traditions (forthcoming)
Greenfire: Making Love With the Goddess
Moonflower: Erotic Dreaming With the Goddess
The Pocket Guide to Celtic Spirituality
The Pocket Guide to Crystals and Gemstones
The Shapeshifter Tarot (coauthor)
The Wiccan Web (coauthor, forthcoming)
The Shapeshifter's Handbook (forthcoming)

LOVE, SEX, AND MAGICK

*Exploring the Spiritual Union
Between Male and Female*

SIRONA KNIGHT

A Citadel Press Book
Published by Carol Publishing Group

A Citadel Press Book
Published by Carol Publishing Group
Citadel Press is a registered trademark of Carol Communications, Inc.

Editorial, sales and distribution, and rights and permissions inquiries should be addressed
to Carol Publishing Group, 120 Enterprise Avenue, Secaucus, N.J. 07094.

In Canada: Canadian Manda Group, One Atlantic Avenue, Suite 105,
Toronto, Ontario M6K 3E7

Carol Publishing Group books may be purchased in bulk at special discounts for sales
promotion, fund-raising, or educational purposes. Special editions can
be created to specifications. For details, contact Special Sales Department,
Carol Publishing Group, 120 Enterprise Avenue, Secaucus, N.J. 07094.

Manufactured in the United States of America
10 9 8 7 6 5 4 3 2 1

Library of Congress Cataloging-in-Publication Data
Knight, Sirona, 1955–
Love, sex, and magick : exploring the spiritual union between male
and female / Sirona Knight.
p.   cm.
Includes bibliographical references and index.
ISBN 0–8065–2043–4 (pbk.)
1. Love—Miscellanea. 2. Sex—Miscellanea. 3. Magic. I. Title.
BF1623.L6K57   1998
133.4′3—dc21   98–52835
CIP

This book is dedicated to Michael,
who is my fire, water, earth, and air,
and to Skylor, our bright son.

And to all the people in the world who dare
to create positive love, sex, and magick
in their daily lives.

CONTENTS

ॐ

APPENDIXES

ACKNOWLEDGMENTS

I would like to express my never-ending thanks and love to Michael and Skylor for their eternal love, light, and laughter. And a special thank you to my family, friends, students, and everyone who has been so supportive in the writing of this book. Eternal thanks to the Goddesses and Gods for their friendship and love, and for helping me every moment of my life.

I would also like to particularly acknowledge and thank Mike Lewis, my editor at Carol Publishing, for his patience, sense of humor, and continued faith in my writing abilities. And a special thank you to Steven Schragis of Carol Publishing for his support, enthusiasm, and for keeping such an open mind.

I would like to acknowledge and thank Jerry Snider for his friendship, confidence in me, and sharp wit, and Michael Langevin for his encouragement and support, and all the folks at *Magical Blend* magazine for their help. A heartfelt thanks to everyone at *New Age Retailer* magazine, especially Molly Trimble for her upbeat sense of humor, kind words, and enthusiasm, and Duane Sweeney for his continued support. I would also like to express my deep appreciation to Dan Liss at *Aquarius* magazine for his friendship and understanding, and to Ailette Rodriguez at *Wiccan Times* for her sensitivity and support.

A special acknowledgement and loving thank you to Patricia Telesco for everything, especially her friendship and for opening the door to new adventures, and to Dorothy Morrison for her humor and friendship. I would also like to respectfully. thank James Redfield, Neale Donald Walsch, John Perkins, and Michael Garrett, as well as Margo Anand, Dr. John Gray, and Judith Orloff, for the work they are doing to heal the earth and create a brighter future for humankind. Also many blessings and thanks to John Nelson for his creative vision, friendship, and continued encouragement.

Much love and many thanks to Melissa Dragich Merritt for her generosity. Also, kind and loving thanks to Lady Maireid Sullivan for her friendship and beautiful music. Blessings and thanks to Robbie Robertson for speaking out against oppression and for his incredible music. I also would like to express my never-ending appreciation to Donovan for his kindness and inspiring songs. And many thanks to an extraordinary drummer, Barrett Martin, for creating such sacred and magickal dimensions with his hands and heart.

Bright blessings and love to A. J. Drew at Salem West in Columbus, Ohio, for his friendship, support, and the work he is doing to help people understand the positive wisdom of Wicca. May the Goddess and God bless MoonRaven and DragonHawk at Whispered Prayers in Chico, California, for their support and friendship. Also, bright blessings and thanks to everyone at Triple Moon for their enthusiasm and intelligent conversation.

I would like to acknowledge and sincerely thank each one of you for encouraging me to continue on the Great Adventure.

Blessed Be! Blessed Be the Gods!

INTRODUCTION

ॐ

Love, Sex, and Magick is about the union of female and male energies and how this union can be loving, sexual, and magickal all at the same time. A relationship between two people, by its very nature, raises some basic and universal questions. Who are they and what are their individual needs? What form of interaction or relationship do they desire with one another? How can their relationship evolve and become more sacred? The six chapters of *Love, Sex, and Magick* will offer suggestions on how you can answer these questions in your life, as well as include examples and guidelines for more fulfilling relationships.

Any relationship, whether sexual, intellectual, or spiritual, involves the balancing and integration of polarities of energies. Because of this, many of the concepts presented in *Love, Sex, and Magick* are universal and can be applied to many types of relationships, even though the focus of the book is on love relationships. The balancing and integration of female and male polarities is not limited to relationships between women and men, even though the examples used in the book involve this type of relationship. These concepts apply to most relationships—heterosexual, bisexual, homosexual, monogamous, and polygamous.

PART I

کس

LOVE

T he initial step to finding someone to love is to first understand who you are as a person. The following section on love includes steps for looking at all your qualities and determining what you need and desire from a relationship. By knowing and learning to love yourself, you begin opening up, like the petals of a flower, to the feelings of love, which are like the light and warmth of the sun.

Once you understand who you are as a person, you are then ready to take steps toward ascertaining potential partners and types of relationships. Chapter 2 provides instructions for drawing up a personality profile, including listing characteristics you like in another person. This technique helps you start seeing this prospective partner in more definitive terms.

Equal in importance to knowing yourself is making the effort and taking the time to know the many aspects of your potential partner. You must be honest with yourself, because the more honest you are, the better your chance for a successful and fulfilling relationship, regardless of the type you seek. Avoid deceiving yourself about your chosen partner, and don't cover up something that doesn't feel right, because the deception will later arise in the relationship.

The next step involves choosing the kind of relationship you want. Basically, each person's needs must be met on some level, or an imbalance in the relationship will always be present. By knowing yourself and your needs, and the other person and his or her needs, you begin to see how a relationship works, and, in turn, doesn't work. This perception gives you insights and helps you choose the most appropriate kind of relationship.

Also, this choice doesn't have to be permanent. If you desire, you can change the nature of the relationship anytime, in such ways as becoming more intimate and deepening the bond between you and your partner.

Once you have decided the nature of the relationship, the time comes to create and build it. In intimate relationships, the essential ingredients of imagination, wonder, and open discussion occupy an important part. Additionally, each person must have the space to grow and reach their fullest potential for the exchange to be successful and beneficial for each partner. Through time and the aid of words and actions, the relationship and the energetic bond strengthens, building love and trust.

When cooking, spices enhance the flavor of food. In relationships, love, sex, and magick act to add to the exchange between lovers, creating depth and eventually a boundless nature to the relationship. *Love, Sex and Magick* draws from many sources, whose diversity extends from tantra to the Celtic Druid tradition. Using these sources, lovers can add new dimensions to their interactions, whether spiritual, intellectual, or sexual. Once again, the intention is the coming together of female and male polarities into a harmonious mixture.

In the ancient Celtic myth of Tristan and Isolt, the lovers drink a potion that sends them into frenzied passion for four years, at which point the potion wears off. In relationships, the test of time becomes both partners evolving together so that their interaction continues to empower them simultaneously on many levels. The connection between individuals can extend beyond this plane to include the spiritual bonding of souls that continually meet in other lifetimes, working out energetic polarities that transcend the barriers of mortal lifetimes.

In Upanishadic philosophy, whose roots connect to tantra, *purusha,* the human spirit, stays in a state of sleep if no desire stirs and no dream is seen. By entering into a spiritual relationship, a person embraced by a loving partner knows no distinction of other and self, which is synonymous with the human spirit knowing no distinction between itself and the divine. This essentially conveys the idea behind the spiritual relationship.

This doesn't mean giving up yourself and who you are for the relationship, but more for the idea of the three faces—female, male, and neutral balance—which all give form to the many aspects of the relationship. The balance, rather than a place where you lose yourself, is instead a place where you become more in touch with your many faces.

The intention of *Love, Sex, and Magick* is to provide a framework for having successful and lasting relationships. The suggestions contained in the following chapters are intended to guide in the gradual process of gaining freedom and finding meaning through self-improvement and sexual experience. It is the process of moving from being essentially directed by others to becoming self-directed, listening to your inner voice, merging with Oneness, and finding the pattern for the lifestyle you desire.

1

The Myths and Legends
of Romance and Love

It's still the same old story
A fight for love and glory
A case of do or die.
The world will always welcome lovers
As time goes by.

—Herman Hupfeld

Love, according to the ancient Celts, derived first from the perfect love of the Goddess combined with the perfect peace of the God; second, from the perfect love of knowledge and the perfect peace of wisdom; and third, the perfect love of all nature and the perfect peace by being in harmony with all things, animate or inanimate. Each of these concepts convey the idea of the balancing of polarities. Relationships as a whole involve the balancing of a multitude of polarities, from male and female to intuitive and analytical. Each of these seemingly opposite characteristics all stream back into the wholeness of the relationship. This is expressed in the words of the poem "Divine Love," by Michael Starwyn: "You are unto me as I am unto you, and together we form an entity that lives as something within and without ourselves, all part of the divine Oneness."

Legendary Lovers

Our adventure into the myths and legends of romance and love begins with the mythology surrounding some of the great lovers through history, such as Samson and Delilah, Lancelot and Guinevere, and, of course, the ultimate love story, Romeo and Juliet. Each of these lovers and their stories have, through time, taken on mythical qualities, influencing not only how people view love collectively, but also individual perceptions.

A great body of literature and art has found its inspiration in the area of love and romance. William Shakespeare epitomizes this in his plays, such as *Romeo and Juliet,* and also writes about other legendary lovers, such as Mark Anthony and Cleopatra, and Hamlet and Ophelia.

For me, Shakespeare's play *Romeo and Juliet* represents one of the classic tales of romance and love, complete with love at first sight, intense passion, and in the end, tragedy and death. After going back over the play, I was intrigued by how well it symbolized love in *Love, Sex, and Magick.* I was particularly taken by one event which transpires after Romeo and Juliet first meet at a party. Experiencing love at first sight, both lovers have the same reaction to falling in love with someone whom their family disapproves of. The fact that their families are almost at war with each other doesn't help the turbulent situation. This precarious position is summed up by Romeo, who, after seeing and talking with Juliet for the first time, laments that he has unknowingly engaged his heart to his foe. This predicament troubles him greatly, but not so much as to dissuade him from loving his beloved, the fair Juliet.

As for Juliet, she had been suddenly spellbound with the same hasty and inconsiderate passion for Romeo. To her it seemed a prodigious birth of love that she must love her enemy, and that her affections should settle where family considerations should induce her chiefly to hate.

What intrigued me most about this passage was that it expressed the feeling of love moving beyond the normal bounds of time and space to a realm akin to the spiritual. Each of us have had the experience of meeting someone for the first time and sensing an immediate kinship. It feels like you have known the person from somewhere before, suddenly the experience takes on dreamlike qualities, as if transcending to a higher level. These experiences point to the idea that the elements of love, sex, and magick connect and take on new meanings that transcend conventional conceptions of time and space. Each of us, therefore, has the ability to transcend archaic, old-school ideas regarding relationships and enter into a higher state of consciousness.

Love stories permeate the mythology and folklore of every culture, from the Egyptian lovers Isis and Osiris, the Celtic lovers Isolt and Tristan, and the Greek lovers Psyche and Eros, to the Hindu lovers Devi and Shiva. The fascination with love and romance in art and literature is a reflection of our own fascination, as shown by the success and continued popularity of the classic movie *Casablanca,* in which World War II is used as backdrop for a bittersweet love story between the characters Rick and Ilsa, played by Humphrey Bogart and Ingrid Bergman. Bogart reveals to us that love does not conquer all—that often the well-being of the whole is more important than the happiness of a single individual.

Another example of humankind's fascination for tragic love stories is depicted in the recent movie *Titanic,* in which the sinking of a ship becomes the vehicle for a relationship between the two main characters, Rose and Jack, played by Kate Winslet and Leonardo DiCaprio, again involving the mythological elements of romantic attraction, sexual passion, and, in the end, tragedy.

The Mythology of Romance and Love

Much of art, music, literature, history, and spirituality revolve around the themes of romance and love. Just as love and romance influence and inspire art and literature, art and literature create and add to the legends of love and romance, which in turn influence our perceptions and actions. In love—as in sex and magick—the polarities of energy come together as one, and within this union comes an energy and force that is unbridled in its infinite capacity and potential; it is a power than can be directed and harnessed. According to mythology, the coming together of these energies has moved continents, created empires, and built and destroyed armies and cities.

When looking at the effect of mythology on love, it is important to understand the basic nature of mythology and how it influences our conceptions of romance and love. In his book *The Masks of God: Creative Mythology* (see Bibliography), Joseph Campbell describes the function of mythology as reconciling the waking consciousness to the mysteries of the universe, and rendering an interpretive image of this reconciliation that can be understood and integrated into contemporary consciousness. For example, Shakespeare's definition of the function of his art was "to hold as 'twere, the mirror up to nature."

Mythology also reinforces the moral and cultural order of a society. Probably the most significant and critical function of mythology is to facilitate the centering and unfolding of each individual. This process is in accord with yourself (the microcosm), your culture (the mesocosm), the universe (the macrocosm), and that ever-present spiritual mystery that both encompasses all things yet is beyond all things (Oneness).

Myths have a built-in dualistic nature in that by being unverifiable they often seem unbelievable and fantastic—something you look at and then move beyond—and they put you in touch with yourself and the world, giving you a sense of origins, ancestry, history, and inspiring your creativity. In fact, in many ways mythology is much more efficient and effective than history, and certainly more exciting and fascinating.

Myths represent basic archetypes that continually appear in the arts as stories told in new ways, with the basic underlying themes remaining the same. Within each myth is essentially a truth and an untruth, whose combination again invokes dynamic polarity. These two polarities connect together, both to themselves and as components of the whole, representing archetypes for love, sex, and magick.

A mythological example showing the polarity of truth and untruth is the Celtic tale of Tristan and Isolt. They begin their romance when Isolt accidentally drinks a magickal love potion in the presence of Tristan, which induces the two of them to fall blindly and completely in love with each other. Isolt is married to King Mark of Cornwall, and so she and Tristan must resolve their passions secretly. After being discovered by King Mark, Tristan leaves the country. The two lovers are to be reunited in the end, but through treachery they end up like Romeo and Juliet: Tristan kills himself because he thinks Isolt has not returned, and when she sees him dead, she kills herself.

Not a happy ending, this is often typical of myths involving relationships with great passion. Love stories like this seem overly dramatic and basically unbelievable. How many people do you know who take love potions, fall madly in love with the person, and then kill themselves when they find their lover is dead? Many times the initial reaction is to put a myth such as this one in the realm of unreality.

At the same time that you label myth as unreal, your mind and thoughts move in another direction, giving you the subtle message that on some level relationships usually have tragic endings, particularly if they involve love, sex, and magick. Often you absorb this message on an unconscious, archetypal level, even though on this level these messages ultimately have a conscious effect on your personal mythology.

In her book *The Passion of Isis and Osiris: A Union of Two Souls,*

Jean Houston discusses how archetypes work in the context of mythology and relationships: "Quintessentially, archetypes are about relationships. They are the connectiveness for the way things evolve, grow, relate, and become more complex, until they are integrated into the essence of simplicity."

When making an effort to understand love and romance, it is important to think and talk about tendencies rather than rules. People and relationships follow certain patterns, but within these patterns exceptions for every tendency invariably exist. Nonetheless, people tend to repeatedly act in certain ways, particularly in their relations with others. These tendencies are what effect mythology and the legends of romance and love.

The idea of love at first sight, and how this experience transcends physical reality, is another concept of mythology and archetypes that *Romeo and Juliet* exemplifies. Additionally, *Romeo and Juliet* perpetuates the mythology that love has a tragic element to it, and the romantic relations of women and men are traditionally viewed as being calculated, like a game of chess.

Relationships are energetic exchanges. These begin when you meet another person and there are great energetic rivers and streams connecting you in energetic families, monads, totems, and elements. Love at first sight is an ideal played up by literature, but in reality some kind of energetic attraction and connection does take place. This initial exchange is what relationships build upon and what gives them longevity. Many spiritual traditions speak about this underlying energetic connection, which seems surreal and beyond the space-time continuum. This is certainly indicative of what happens when you meet that special someone.

The first time I saw my husband Michael, I was sitting in the lunchroom as a freshman in high school. Suddenly, I looked up and there he was. I couldn't stop staring at him because he seemed so familiar. Going to class after lunch, I was about to walk by him and suddenly, without warning, I saw a huge hand of light coming down from the clouds, pointing directly at him. Very clearly, I heard an inner voice say, "He's the one." For a few moments I paused, as did he, disoriented and feeling like I had been hit by a truck.

Love at first sight also extends into the magickal realm of falling in love with someone you have never met, for example, falling in love with a person's picture. In 1867, Samuel Clemens, also known as Mark Twain, sailed to Europe with Charles Langdon, and in Charles's stateroom was a picture of his sister Olivia. Upon seeing the picture, Samuel immediately fell in love with her. Six months later, he met her and her family in New York City, and two years later Samuel and Olivia were wed. He wrote these words about his relationship: "If given the chance to do it over, I would marry in early infancy instead of wasting time cutting teeth and breaking crockery."

This concept of falling in love with someone you have never met is prevalent throughout folk literature. Besides falling in love by means of a picture, other methods include falling in love upon hearing a person's name, their voice, a description of the person, or by seeing her or him in a dream. An example of the last is the Celtic story of Angus Og and Caer, in which she comes to him every night in his dreams for a year. Having fallen in love with her, he seeks her out and finds she is a swan maiden who was only able to enter his dreams as a human. In the end he becomes a swan, and the lovers are united.

In these stories, the underlying theme is that anytime you meet someone you exchange energy. Love at first sight has to do with polarities of female and male energies that interact on many levels simultaneously, which include the unseen. This integration and connection of female and male energies is at the heart of every relationship. The connection is always there, whether you are immediately aware of it or not. Also, relationships grow stronger over time. This is due to a growing awareness, because as you come to know someone more intimately you become more aware of your connection. In this way, the success of a relationship often directly relates to the intensity of the inherent and natural energetic connections between the individuals involved.

Sexual Polarities

The following Egyptian mythological tale of creation conveys the idea of sexual polarities and how they connect people, while it also talks about the origin of male and female energies.

In the beginning all that existed was the Great He/She, Atum. Perfection not being enough, Atum felt lonely and desired companionship with an Other. Through a union of self with Self, Atum begat two tawny lion-headed children: Shu, the son, became the practical, the mind, the God of air; Tefnut, the daughter, become the passionate, the emotional, the Goddess of moisture.

From these primal beginnings come the energies that are male and female, which are on one hand inherently in opposition to each other. On the other, these two energies are in balance; through love, sex, and magick, the two polarities swing back together as the One, from which they were created, thus connecting and completing the circle.

This concept of sexual polarities also underlies the old saying that "opposites attract." Again, this speaks to the idea that when people meet and enter into a relationship, the connection goes beyond a physical and mental attraction, as is normally perceived, and into a connection that is energetic, moving into the spiritual. By combining the physical and mental together, with energetic, you add another dimension to love and relationships. Body, mind, and spirit come together, as the bonds, connections, and dependencies you build are not only physical and mental, but also energetic and spiritual.

A Technique for Assessing Your Energetic Connections

Because each interaction and relationship is primarily an exchange of energy, becoming aware of your energetic connections with other people and how they effect you on a physical, mental, and spiritual level is vitally important to your well-being. The following technique is useful for assessing your feelings for someone you have just met or someone you have known for a while, including your lover.

Begin by clearing your mind of everything. Take a few deep breaths. With each breath, feel yourself breathing in energy and light and then exhaling all the tasks and concerns of the day. Do this for a few minutes.

Now, in your mind's eye, imagine the person and all of your interactions and connections to him or her. Become aware of as much of your relationship with this person that you can, until the image in your mind becomes as clear as possible.

Ask yourself the following questions. (If you want, you can write down your impressions to review later.) The first question is, how do you feel when you interact with this person? What are your sensations? Are you energized or drained before, during, and after the interaction? Do you feel enriched or depleted? How do you feel and respond, physically, mentally, and spiritually, when you are around this person? How do you feel, on a gut level, when you are around this person? Be aware of higher levels of interaction; the energetic is often unseen, but usually sensed or felt. Do you feel the person is positive, negative, or neutral, active or passive? Do you enjoy the interaction? Why? Do you feel a charge of energy when the person is around?

When you are using this technique, the clearer the image of the person in your mind, the clearer your answers to the questions will be. As much as possible, go with your first impressions and feelings, and when you are done, take all of your answers and impressions and put them into a total perspective. Are the majority of your needs and desires being met, and are you getting what you want from the exchange? The answers to these questions should give you insights into your energetic connections to this person. Also, when you ask these questions it is important to be honest with yourself, because you are only deceiving yourself if you are not. To be blind in love and see someone as you would like them to be, not as they truly are, always leads to unhappiness and hurtful relationships.

The Drama of Love

The dramatic tragic ending is a classic element in the mythology and legends of love and romance. Again, Romeo and Juliet typify this ending, which has been glamorized by literature and culture as something that is normal, when in fact it doesn't have to be.

Literature, by virtue of being literary, looks for the elements of love, adventure, and tragedy. In a desire to make their work stand out as sensational, creative artists often choose the extreme rather than the commonplace. Because of this, tragedy becomes unduly accentuated, both in art and mythology, and people begin to think that all love ends in tragedy. More precisely, love is the balance between two extremes or polarities—female and male, love and hate, passion and indifference.

Everyone has a sense of drama with which they color their world from time to time. It breaks up the monotony and routine of everyday life. Part of this drama involves adding a bittersweet or tragic element to relationships, but if taken too far this tendency can be dangerous because it becomes a self-fulfilling prophecy. Intention is vitally important in relationships, and it is not wise to intend, consciously or subconsciously, for your relationships to be tragic.

Anytime you deal with intense emotions and people's vulnerability, you run the risk of someone's feelings getting hurt. Also, each of us is a living human being and our bodies have a finite life span. Physical death is an inherently tragic element that exists within every relationship and not something any of us really understand. But again, death is a polarity, with the opposite pole being life, happiness, and bliss. As with anything else, you need to balance love and romance between the poles and realize that love occurs on many levels and dimensions. Remember, many of the spiritual bonds and dimensions of relationships do not end with this lifetime.

The essential way to move away from tragic relationships is to build positive patterns, moving your mind and thoughts toward that outcome. Each relationship you enter into has a pattern to it, as does everything in life. By building positive patterns you lessen the possibilities of and tendencies toward painful and tragic relationships.

By staying in the now, being aware, and enjoying each moment as a banquet of experience, you lessen the possibility of tragedy not just in your relationships, but in every aspect of your life. Don't destroy your patterns and relationships because you think subconsciously that relationships never work out and always end in tragedy. By staying in the moment, you can enjoy every moment you spend with your partner. Once you have made a loving and magickal connection with someone, whether for a day or seventy-five years, this experience can never really be tragic because it essentially lives on through eternity, over many lifetimes. It is a connection forever.

No War—Only Polarities

Another aspect of the myths of love revolves around the idea of the war between the sexes. Men and women represent energetic polarities, male and female. When these energies come together in a relationship, they essentially become one, as does all energy. The Celtic image of the perfect love of the Goddess coupled with the perfect peace of the God embodies this union and mating of female and male energies. When the participants in a relationship are at war with one another the conflict may be stimulating, but it is ultimately destructive. The relationship is always a battle or struggle that depletes personal energy and defeats both parties.

In his book *Men Are From Mars, Women Are From Venus* (see Bibliography), Dr. John Gray addresses the issue of the war between the sexes. He recommends that both women and men need to stop offering the method of caring they would prefer and start learning the different ways their partners think, feel, and react. Women have a tendency to positively respond to caring, devotion, and validation, as well as respect, reassurance, and understanding, while men respond to encouragement, appreciation, and trust, as well as admiration, acceptance, and approval. When a woman's attitude toward a man is open and receptive, he feels trusted and needed. To trust a man is to know that he is doing his best. When a woman's reactions reveal positive support of her partner's abilities and intentions, his primary love need is fulfilled, and he is automatically more caring, cooperative, and attentive to her feelings and needs.

The simple act of appreciation reduces a lot of conflict between couples. Appreciation is the natural reaction to being supported. When you feel appreciated, you know your efforts are not wasted and are encouraged to give more. When you feel appreciated, you are empowered and motivated to respect your partner more, and with respect and understanding, your mate feels empowered. When listening to your partner, it's important to remember that an understanding attitude doesn't presume to already know their thoughts, feelings, or motivations. Instead, collect meaning from what you hear, sense, and experience. This validates what your lover is communicating and avoids a great deal of conflict and misunderstanding.

Unfortunately, in the culturalized and conditional war between the sexes, love and romance have become a complicated game of chess, typified by Jane Austen novels such as *Pride and Prejudice* and *Emma*. Modern cinemagraphic examples include movies such as *First Wives' Club* and *The Ref.* In the game of love, men and women act like players whose motivation is to influence and attract potential mates. *Romeo and Juliet* sums up this game well when, as Juliet stands out on the balcony, a crimson blush comes over her face, which Romeo cannot see because of the night. Upon reflecting her love for Romeo, which she had intended, she would have recanted her words, but that was impossible. Had she been able, she would have stood upon form and kept her lover at a distance. This is the custom of discreet ladies, to frown and be perverse, and give their suitors harsh denials at first. By being standoffish and affecting coyness or indifference, women make their lovers think they are elusive and not too easily won, for the difficulty of attainment increases the value of an object. Hence the saying, She says no when she really means yes.

People are not objects, in relationships or otherwise. That they are is an old-school and obsolete way of thinking and utter nonsense. The "hard to get" approach is just a game, which may be fun to play for a time, but ultimately perpetuates a stagnant point of view and sets up a contradiction that keeps playing out again and again. Relationships work best when no means no, yes means yes, and the people involved are able to clearly communicate their likes and dislikes to each other.

Supporting and strengthening one another is an important aspect of any successful relationship. The interaction should empower both people. With the reemergence of Goddess energy, women are finally realizing and owning their personal power. Men are also realizing their own power, as well as being able to express certain qualities that were traditionally regarded as feminine. Instead of being a struggle and a battle, a relationship can empower both people, for working together accomplishes much more and provides more enriching life experiences. We also become whole people—physically, emotionally, and spiritually.

In terms of love, romance, and relationships, myths and legends portray something that is both real and beyond real, which speaks again of inherent polarities. It is our energetic connection with another human being that makes or breaks the relationship. If the exchange is mutually beneficial in terms of satisfying the needs and desires of both partners, then there is a foundation for a successful relationship. This infers a balance of energies and polarities, involving all aspects of love, sex, and magick.

2

Discovering and Rediscovering Your Lover

Following the flight of birds
we see the sky more clearly
how horizon may join two worlds
the way a bird joins the sky
the way trees join the earth
the way we join each other.

—June Sylvester

Discovering your lover is an initial step in building an intimate relationship. The beauty of this process is that it never ends because as you delve deeper, you keep rediscovering your lover at every level, reaching toward the divine.

Each partner within a relationship represents an energetic polarity, and how well a relationship works reflects the integration and balance of the energetic polarities between people. This concept of polarities is beautifully expressed by Plato in his classical work,

Symposium, in which he describes how each person is at one time two selves united into one. At a certain point, these two selves become separated, and because of this people spend their lives looking for their other half. When the two selves find one another there is an instant recognition. In terms of a relationship, the circle is complete and whole again.

Intimacy

Modern society encourages and praises people as they become more efficient rather than more intimate. The current trend keeps moving toward more mechanical relationships, both with the world and other people. Mechanical, in terms of a sexual relationship, means that things become rote and take on a mundane, routine quality. Intimacy breaks up this mechanical element in that it deepens the bond between two people on all levels: body, mind, and spirit.

Raising your level of intimacy with another person can, at first, seem like a frightening prospect, but the rewards for your relationship are astronomical. The frightening part comes from having to let down your built-up boundaries and defenses, allowing another person to know you on an intimate level. The joyous rewards stem from bonding with your partner, and in the process deepening your connection as two physical, sexual, and spiritual beings. (Bonding is a necessary part of establishing an intimate relationship. If you do not bond, you never make it to the level of true intimacy.)

The word intimacy stems from the Latin word *inter,* meaning "within." Our intimate relationships are those that affect our innermost feelings and being. Intimacy means moving beyond physical closeness to allowing yourself to be yourself in the relationship. When you bond with the essence of another and the nature of all things, you open a door that also allows you a deeper understanding of yourself.

Intimacy begins with your relationship with yourself. Trying to find intimacy with another person is impossible when you begin with alienation and division within yourself. If you cannot be open and honest with yourself, you cannot expect to be able to be honest with someone else—friend, family member, or lover. Self-honesty is the first step to intimacy and the cornerstone in building an intimate relationship, because once you are honest with yourself and your true feelings, needs, and wants, you open the door to deepening your relationship with your partner.

As a child you learn to begin walling off your true feelings and building boundaries that let no one in, including yourself. We do this to avoid dealing with our feelings. Once you become an adult, the walls and boundaries are so tightly in place that the notion of ever letting them down is downright frightening. At this point, you become out of touch and disconnected with yourself, with little chance of moving beyond this point for fear of the real you that might be found within the walls. Fear becomes your main obstacle to intimacy.

Personal Mythology and Intimacy

As discussed in chapter 1, there exists a mythology about love and romance that plays heavily into your feelings about what a sexual relationship should be. Part of becoming intimate with yourself is delving into and familiarizing yourself with your personal mythology, which is formed by the combination of socialization and personal experiences. Exploring your own attitudes about relationships enables you to become intimate with who you are, particularly in terms to your expectations and behavior patterns.

Your personal mythology about love is an essential element to examine when assessing yourself in terms of relationships, with your past the basis for your personal mythology. This is your conditioning. On a personal level, past experiences and situations become a living mythology, with experience driving your belief systems. If you have had negative experiences in relationships, especially intimate ones, you will most likely continue to experience these problems unless you change your pattern. Likewise, if you have had successful relationships you will probably continue to do so.

Personal mythology also has a positive aspect in that you can learn from your past relationships, and in doing so evolve your understanding of both relationships and yourself. By looking back and seeing what has worked for you in the past, you begin to sense your realistic needs and desires in a relationship. Accentuate the positive ones, which are your strengths, while moving past and minimizing the negative, which are your weaknesses. The main idea is to concentrate on the positive and your strengths.

When looking at yourself and assessing your personal mythology with respect to relationships, try to observe your strengths and weaknesses as an observer, with impartiality. The more honest you are with yourself, the better your chance of having a relationship that fulfills your needs and is more likely to succeed in the long run.

You have multiple personalities that are integrated into who you are. These multiple qualities are important when understanding your needs and desires within a relationship. You may experience times when you need space, and because of this want to be left alone. At other times you may feel romantic and full of wild passion. These two very different needs have to be satiated for you to be whole. If you cut yourself off from aspects of yourself, you again set up a problematic pattern. It is much healthier and more pleasant to explore and satisfy your desires in a relationship with a loving partner.

Self-discovery

Personal intimacy and self-discovery imply looking within and going beneath the surface. By being in tune with yourself and your inner voice, you begin to trust your instincts and perceptions. As you become more clear as to who you are, you gain clarity and begin to understand what it takes for you to have a successful relationship. In addition, increased self-awareness also strengthens your connection to a higher spiritual power. When you increase this connection, you proportionately increase the level of synchronicity (i.e. the occurrence of events that connect and relate to each other) in your life. Your dreams and meditations start to take on an almost magickal quality, which spreads to other areas of your life.

In a relationship, it's important to look yourself in the mirror and realistically assess your strong and weak points. What you give to and what you need from a relationship are two questions whose answers have a strong impact on a successful relationship. By working on your weak areas and accentuating your strong points, you can add flavor to the scope and longevity of your relationship. If you decide to alter yourself to fit a particular relationship, remember that ultimately you have to be happy in the situation. It is easier to alter what is there and use your natural proclivities, than to try to make drastic changes and complete a personal makeover. In the long run you will be happier, and your relationship will be much more successful.

Some techniques you can use for self-discovery include meditation, dream work, writing your perceptions and experiences out on paper or in a journal, and creative visualization. When meditating, using a personal mantra or a more generic version, be clear as to what you want from the meditation. In this case, you want to both explore and fine-tune your perception and awareness of yourself.

You can also use dream work to improve your self-awareness. First, you can begin your dream with a meditation or suggestion for a particular type of dream; second, by interpreting the dream afterward you can gain valuable insights into your own personality.

I suggest you get a notebook and begin writing down things about yourself, such as what things make you feel good, particularly when interacting with other people. Are you quiet, shy, and reserved in social situations, or talkative, gregarious, and outspoken? You may find that the answers to these questions differ depending on your mood, which again reflects the multiple faces or aspects of yourself.

A Technique for Self-discovery

This technique requires three sheets of notebook paper and a pen or pencil. Start by sitting down or reclining, relaxing, and getting into a meditative and contemplative state of mind. First, think about the things you do in a day. How do you begin your morning? If you go to work, what do you do at work? What do you do on your lunch hour? What do you do when you get home? Do you watch TV, read, do volunteer work, talk on the telephone, play a musical instrument, write poetry, or engage in some form of sporting activity? Once you have a feel for what you do daily, take one of the pieces of paper and begin writing down your daily activities. Then write down the things you do occasionally, such as taking trips or vacations, going out to dinner, or attending a play or concert. Once you've finished writing, stop and look at all of the things you have written down. What you do is a definite indication of who you are. By looking over this list, you should get more of a feel for who you are.

Next, meditate on the things that appeal to you. What clothes do you prefer to wear? What types of movies do you enjoy watching? What foods do you like to eat? What are your tastes in music, art, and books? What is your concept of a dream home or ideal living situation? What are your spiritual preferences? Once you have all the things you like firmly fixed in your mind, take the second piece of paper, draw a line down the middle of the page, and on the left side of the sheet list the things you like in life.

Once you are finished, sit back and begin thinking about the things you dislike, using the same criteria as before, only in reverse. What type of music, art, movies, books, and foods do you dislike? The reason for meditating on the things you dislike is that sometimes you may not know what you like, while you usually know exactly what you don't like, and knowing what you don't like can give you insights and point you toward what you do like. When you're done meditating on the things you dislike, write them down on the right side of the paper. When finished, look over the two lists before setting the paper down next to the first paper listing things you do. Side by side, the information on these pages should give you more insight into who you are as a person.

Two suggestions for giving more focus to these lists is to take the first page and go down the list of things you do, marking which of these things you prefer doing and which you dislike doing. Now take the second page of likes and dislikes, and mark each item accordingly: 1, I feel very strongly about it; 2, I like it; 3, I could live with or without it.

For the third part of this exercise, meditate on who you are in a relationship. Some of the questions you might ask include: Are you easygoing? Controlling? Organized? An optimist or pessimist? Are you a tactile person who needs a lot of touching? Do you need and/or give a lot of space to others? Are you a very sexual person, and if so, what are your sexual needs and desires? How do you deal with a crisis? Do you anger easily? How do you deal with your anger? Are you active or passive? All of these, and any others you may add, are questions about who you are in a relationship. In other words, what kind of lover are you?

Now, on the third sheet of paper, write all these things down, and after looking it over place it next to the other two sheets. What you have is a three-dimensional glimpse of your personality. From here you can take additional steps, such as, when looking at the list of things you do, if you found that you don't enjoy some of them you might want to take steps toward changing them into things you prefer doing. Also, many books, tapes, and workshops available under the heading "Self-help" can guide you in personal change and self-improvement. For now, the idea of using this technique is to give you a clearer picture and more of a feel for who you are as a person and what kind of lover you are in a relationship.

The Intimate Relationship

Within a relationship, true intimacy is only possible when both partners let down their boundaries. Intimacy cannot be achieved if only one person lowers her boundaries and the other does not. This will result in a control issue. When control and power are at stake, there is no room for intimacy.

Once two people have gone through the process of self-discovery, which includes being in tune with their needs and desires, they are ready to begin an intimate relationship. Inti-macy occurs on physical, mental, and spiritual levels, with experiences such as love, sex, and magick touching and transcending all levels.

Discovering and rediscovering your lover is something that continually happens as the two of you arouse and fine-tune your senses and awareness of each other. Long conversations discussing dreams and desires for the future, moments spent in flesh-to-flesh touching, and lifetimes lived as two souls connected through an eternal and infinite bond often felt on a psychic, if not conscious level, are ways you can become more intimate with your lover. Each experience, when intimate, takes on qualities that are without a doubt magickal. At times, we may think we have an infinite bond with another and ultimately discover we are wrong. This is all part of the learning process we all go through in our search for magickal love.

When I first met my husband Michael, I felt an energetic connection that bridged multiple lifetimes. Our intimacy came through long conversations in which we revealed our innermost thoughts and became best friends. Our intimacy extends into both our sexual and spiritual relationship, and even after twenty-eight years I still feel an energetic charge every time we make contact. The electricity is still there, and our relationship has become a sensual experience that seems to grow and flower over time.

Sexual Intimacy

You are not alone or isolated from your world, but intimately connected to and subtly affected by everyone and everything around you. When you join together with another person and share your visions and dreams, higher levels of healing and coherence are possible. In this way, you can actually formulate a pattern for the reality you desire. In terms of sexual intimacy, this takes a multitude of forms and represents states ranging from lust to reassurance, all the way to comfort and spiritual bonding. Sexual intimacy is a way of making love to intimately reconnect with your lover, while acting out mutual caring.

Sexual intimacy comes from finding forms of expression that touch the soul. When you make love with someone with whom you have a spiritual bond, one which moves beyond the physical and mental to a higher state, you add dimension and depth to your sexual experience. When you see your reflection in another person, for a moment you become one, and even if this moment is only for an instant it is still an instant of unforgettable divine intimacy.

Rather than being only a physical or mechanical experience, making love with someone can extend into the spiritual depth that awakens when you merge with the soul of the other person. The magickal language of touch opens up deeper levels of sexual intimacy. When you and your lover become silent and begin communicating through touch, you convey emotions and feelings that move beyond the boundaries of words. In one sense touch is a physical sensation, and in another, it is an energetic experience in which your and your lover's energies intertwine, spirit to spirit.

When communicating and connecting with your lover, you give added dimension to your sexual intimacy by utilizing all of your senses. When bathing together or giving each other a massage, using a scented oil, such as rose or vanilla, deepens the experience. Lighting candles and playing music that you both connect to are other ways to become more sexually intimate. These and other methods are covered in detail in the sections on Sex and Magick, and the appendices in the back of the book, which give instructions for candle magick, and listings for using different magickal oils, as well as stones, herbs, flowers, and resins, for greater sexual intimacy.

Using Creative Visualizations for Intimacy

One way to establish and increase intimacy with your lover is through creative visualization. Visualization describes the way we communicate from our mind to our body. It is the process of shaping thoughts and images in our mind and then transmitting them to the body as signals or desires.

The foundation of creative visualization is the imagination, which is the ability to create an idea, mental picture, or image in your mind. By using your imagination it becomes possible to reach out to areas of knowledge that are physically absent. In doing so you can begin to use this knowledge to enhance your relationships, with yourself and others.

We are our images. Form follows thought, so your image of yourself forms your picture of reality. In creative visualization, imagination and imagery are used to create a clear image of something you desire in your life and wish to achieve. Bear in mind that a strong imagination can generate an actual event. Accordingly, if you wish to accomplish something in tangible reality, it is essential that you first picture yourself achieving it in your imagination.

Your perception and other processes are channeled by the ways you anticipate events and experience. You are the summation of your perceptions. Creative visualization works through systematically and repeatedly seeing and sensing yourself making the wisest choices and selecting the "path with a heart" that is right for you. Follow that which you love, for that is your destiny. If you make an effort to do this, you will find there is generally a predictable transfer from imagery to reality. Remember, the more powerful and real the image, the more effective the chance for personal growth and change.

Most people rely heavily on their sense of vision and find creative visualization (the means to creating and manifesting goals and experiences) an easy and enjoyable method for personal exploration and change. Keep in mind that it is not necessary to mentally see an image when doing creative visualization. For those who are not visually oriented, creative visualization acts primarily as thoughts or even sensations, rather than as actual mind pictures. All approaches are acceptable as long as they create the eventual outcome you desire.

A Creative Visualization: The Intimate Journey

Begin by closing your eyes and breathing deeply, feeling more relaxed with each breath. Settle into your chair or recline, getting as comfortable as you can. Allow your breath to carry you into a slowly moving stream, where each breath continues to flow over you, relaxing you even more.

Breathe in to the count of three, holding your breath for three counts and then exhaling completely. Do this three times or more, deeply breathing in and out and relaxing more and more, just allowing all of the tensions, stresses, and worries of the day to move out of your body every time you exhale. Every sound you hear in the room just helps you to relax further, as you feel your being becoming calm, relaxed, and peaceful.

Begin to breathe white light into your body from all around you. Also feel yourself breathing in the light through your skin, softly and completely. As you breathe in, you can feel the light flowing through your body and warming your entire being as everything melts into One.

Now, very slowly begin to visualize yourself walking down a garden path on a warm summer's night. The full moon is shining, the air is warm, and a gentle breeze kisses your face. You come to a garden gate, which is very ornate, decorated with the faces of animals along with the shapes of flowers and trees. All of these images are fashioned into the intricate ironwork. You slowly open the gate.

As you open the gate, you notice the reflection of the moon's milky light on the skin of your hands. You walk slowly through the gate into the garden, leaving it open behind you. Upon entering the lush garden, you smell the fragrant aroma of roses, lavender, and jasmine, which fills your senses with delight.

Walking on, you hear the sound of frogs, crickets, and birds as they create a natural symphony with a rhythm and melody that emanate from the divine energy and soul of the garden. The smell of water greets you as you come to a small pool of water fed by a natural spring. The spring bubbles softly over several large milky white quartz stones as it flows into the garden pool.

You sit down comfortably on the grassy bank next to the pool and look into the still water. You can see the reflection of the moon and yourself in the brightly lit pool. When you dip your hand into the water, the cool, moist sensation lingers on your fingers, spreading to your lips as you drink from the fresh waters of the pool.

You feel completely relaxed and filled with peaceful moonlight. You look over and notice some small white quartz stones on the edge of the pool, and you pick up three stones in your hand and begin throwing them into the pool, one at a time. Each time you watch the ripples move outward and finally disappear you see a face becoming clearer and clearer on the surface of the pool. It may be a face that is familiar or someone you have never met. As you toss in the second stone, the image becomes even more clear.

As you toss the third stone upon the waters, you see a pattern to the ripples, and when they subside they become the moon, which then transforms into the face of your lover. As you stare into your beloved's eyes, you feel your two souls become one.

Rising up from the water, your lover takes your hand. Further down the garden path, the two of you stroll until you come to a giant oak tree that stands with its thick branches reaching up to the sky. You each press both of your hands to the moss-covered base of the tree, and feel its ancient energy and knowledge flowing into you.

In a patch of wild grass at the base of the oak tree, you and your lover lie down next to one another. You feel your bodies begin as two, then transform into one, before becoming two again. Your minds meld into a place where communication is carried out on a nonverbal level. When your souls connect, you feel a completeness.

Moving clockwise around the base of the oak, you chant these words three times in unison with your lover:

> *As one, we became two,*
> *energies different as day from night.*
> *As two, we become one again,*
> *connecting in the infinite web of light,*
> *Ayea, Ayea, Ayea!*

After the third time, you begin to drift out of the visualization, remembering your intimate connection to your lover. Slowly you come completely back to the present moment, but at the same time remembering the sensations, thoughts, and impressions of your intimate journey.

As you conclude the Love section, your journey takes you into the next section, Sex. Love, sex, and magick, like body, mind, and spirit, are forces that play within relationships. Love is a mental activity, dealing with our perceptions of beauty, whereas sex is a physical activity that invokes our primal needs. As you move further along, into the areas of sex and magick, you need to bring the elements of love forward.

PART II

SEX

P rimal eroticism embodies the beginnings of life—cells contracting and expanding to produce regeneration and life. Each of us, as life forms, reproduce this effect in love and sex. As with everything having to do with love, sex, and magick, this phenomenon of expansion and contraction can be understood in terms of energetic polarities, and when these polarities become one you experience divine overtones.

Sexual energy is one of the most potent energies in relationships. The ancients considered sexual intercourse sacred, providing an avenue to enlightenment and deity. Today, humanity needs to move toward freer sexual expression in such a way that encourages wisdom and love rather than control, conflict, and fear. Gathering, generating, directing, and releasing sexual energy is an essential part of being human, which, when fully realized, is truly divine, with all puns intended. This divine sexual experience completely and permanently transforms you and your perceptions of relationships and reality.

Love, sex, and magick work in tandem to create much more than their individual component parts. Sexual activity and expression needs to be seen as something empowering. When you make love, you create a vast amount of positive energy, and this can be used to promote the patterns and perceptions you desire. And it can be used to heal yourself, others, and the world.

Part 2, Sex, first deals with the basic nature of energy in the form of kundalini, and then goes through ways in which this energy can be optimized in the sexual experience. By awakening your kundalini energy and moving the light up through your chakras during sex, you connect with your lover in such a way that can only be identified as sacred, magickal, and divine. This boundless source of energy can then be used to enrich every aspect of your life.

3

Exploring Sexual Energy and Kundalini

I like my body when you hover over me
in this fragile darkness
It is as if the moon lingers above in sweet,
suspended honey
lighting the empire of flesh
the garden of wild roses
that makes up
us together.

—Laura Kennedy

As with love, sexual energy involves polarities. Sex is one of those places where physical and spiritual love meet and become one. When female and male energies unite, the sexual experience becomes intense, with spiritual overtones. The normal constraints of time and space fall away as the experience transports lovers to new heights of ecstacy.

The yin-yang concept, in which the female is yin and the male is yang, stems from the basic concept that balance is the law of existence. The spiritual philosophy of Lamaism takes this theory further when it says that the sexual union is the highest balance of which humankind is capable—unity in opposition. This concept is represented by the symbol of the circle bisected by a sine wave.

Sexual Energy

Sex is good for your health. Sexual arousal activates your endocrine system, which enhances your immune system, slows aging, elevates your moods and emotions, and improves your overall cardiovascular health. In addition, a fulfilling sex life often improves your appearance, helps to keep you fit, and often reduces stress and anxiety. By tapping into your inner wisdom and the natural healing abilities of your body via your sexual response and breath, you can enhance your overall health.

Generating higher levels of sexual energy provides a means for clearing blocked energetic pathways in your body. Sexual energy, which derives from the same divine source as healing energy and life force, can be directed toward areas in your body that are weak.

When you are in close proximity to another person, your energy fields overlap and interpenetrate one another, creating a subtle state of communion. When you are close to another person, such as your lover and spiritual partner, your minds actually become energetically interconnected because you are immersed in each other's energy fields. A kind of direct communication and merging exists between you and your mate that transcends and goes beyond mere interaction through your senses.

Two people create a shared energetic field when concentrating their attention on each other, and this field transcends the traditional perceptions of physical space. An example of this energetic field can be seen in the relationships between women and men of the late-century Yuki Indians of Northern California. When the men of the tribe were away fighting, the women at home did not sleep. They danced continually in a circle, chanting and waving leafy wands, because they felt that if they danced all the time and did not sleep their husbands would not grow tired and would be victorious. Basically, the women were using intention to move the energetic field they had with the men so that it stretched out over physical distances.

Simple examples of participating in these types of experiences are distance healing, telepathy between two or more people, shared dreaming with lovers, family, or friends, as well as prayer and divine communication, déjà vu, and seeing ancestors or ghosts. The fact that these experiences do occur suggests you can alter, intercept, and bend states and forms of energy, such as time, space, and perception. This forms the basis of sympathetic magick.

A person's energy either empowers you with a feeling of positivity or drains you, leaving you feeling negative, agitated, uneasy, or invaded. By becoming aware of which people around you empower you and which do not, you can begin to surround yourself with those who contribute to your well-being and forward movement.

Additionally, research indicates that your autonomic nervous system can indeed be affected by the thoughts or intentions of others—including someone staring at you. This is termed alleo-biofeedback.

As the highest harmonic, sex with someone you love creates coherence, which is the basis for many health benefits. The reason why you can be so moved by being in the presence of someone who radiates genuine love is that the most coherent oscillator, in this case someone oscillating love, tends to pull those around it into entrainment. Additionally, each of your individual cells are oscillators. When you make love with intention, you oscillate collectively with your partner and become one large oscillator.

Whenever you touch another person, an exchange of energy takes place between the two of you. Touch itself communicates energetic information and influences your personal energy field. As you hold hands with someone you are fond of, your heart energies comingle and you actually affect the other person's brain waves, as they do yours.

Many acts of physical intimacy, such as kissing and sexual intercourse, involve moisture, and moisture conducts electricity. These acts allow for a strong exchange of electromagnetic energy. This is one reason why people find certain partners more electrifying than others.

Methods for Directing Energy

Method 1: Giving and Receiving

This method will help you and your partner learn to direct the flow of energy, which is particularly useful during lovemaking as a form of sex magick. One of the most helpful tips in this practice is to use deep rhythmic breathing to facilitate your experience. Begin by sitting comfortably, facing your lover and looking directly at each other, with your hands in the air, palms out. Move your hands toward your partner's slowly, without touching. Feel the energy radiating between your hands. Keep gazing into each other's eyes and breathing deeply during the entire experience. Make an effort to synchronize your breathing. As you continue to stare into your lover's eyes, you may sense some deeper truth or connection beneath their gaze. During this experience, your partner's face may seem to shift shape or become illuminated. These are all normal responses to the energy exchange you are undergoing.

Next, sense your right hand sending energy and your left hand receiving it, and have your partner do likewise. Feel yourself drawing energy from your lover's right hand and then sending it back with your right. Use your imagination to visualize and sense a circular circuit of powerful energy flowing between the two of you. Allow the energy to flow down your right arm and out through your hand, into your lover. Now feel it circulating back around to you and up your left arm, and then into your heart area, moving out again through your right arm and hand. Build the energy slowly as it flows through you both.

After about ten minutes, use your intention and power of mind to reverse the direction of the energy flow, drawing in through your right side and releasing out your left. After a couple of minutes, change the flow once again. Once you have mastered changing the direction of the energy, make an effort to still it, bringing it to rest at the palms of your hands and then bringing it to rest within your heart chakra.

If you are working solo, you can use a quartz crystal held between both hands, circulating the energy in the same manner, right sending and left receiving for a few minutes, and then switching directions, finally stabilizing the energy. Instead of gazing at another person, use a mirror and stare into your own mirrored face.

This method is a very powerful and transformational tool. Once you have experienced this level of consciousness and awareness, everything in your life permanently alters. Your perspective on yourself, others, and the nature of sexual energy, and energy in general, changes forever.

Method 2: Love Energy Visualization

Center yourself and call in any divine energies, Goddesses and Gods, power animals, or ancestors to help and guide you. Close your eyes and visualize a bright, warm white sphere of light surrounding you as you begin thinking about your lover. Breathe deeply, counting to three, holding your breath for three counts and then breathing out completely. As you are breathing in this way, visualize and sense all of the energy that surrounds you moving through your skin and into your body. Actually visualize and sense your body drawing in light. Do this at least three times.

Next, visualize and sense every aspect of your lover—her or his eyes, face, body, mannerisms, voice—filling in all the details you can think of. Allow yourself to receive all the love this person has for you, drawing in their loving feelings, thoughts, and actions. See and sense their love flowing into you like a wave of warm golden light. Feel yourself being filled by their love and light. After a few minutes, when the influx and flow of love has stopped, continue to the next step.

Begin to send that loving energy back to your lover no matter where he or she is—in the same room, at the store, at work, or oceans away. Visualize and sense yourself sending golden light and warm loving thoughts of love to your mate. Use your breath to direct and release your loving energy.

After a few minutes, center your attention and focus on a particular Goddess, God, divine presence, or ancestor. Once again, feel all of the love this being has for you. Willingly let this love in and receive the loving flow of energy they have to offer you. Receive all of their love, using your breath to drink in the energy, drawing it in through your skin, into your body, and finally into your very core. When the influx of love stops, proceed.

Return your loving thoughts and energy to the same Goddess, God, ancestor, or divine presence. See and sense yourself directing and releasing a wave of energy to them. Take a few minutes to breathe deeply and gently, allowing all of your love to flow to the divine being. Then thank them for their love, kindness, and kinship.

When you finish, open your eyes slowly. Finally, give yourself the suggestion to make an effort to hold on to the sense of being loved and of loving throughout the day. Let the love energize and motivate you.

Kundalini

In tantra, the term *sakti* describes the moment when female and male energies come together as one. Essentially an archetype of life itself, mythology depicts this concept in terms of a man coming across a woman kneeling beside a pool of water, and in the reflection he sees, not simply any woman but, with a shock of recognition, exactly and fully this one, thus transforming his perception of love. This transformation involves moving away from viewing this woman as merely present in time and space to an experience that includes perceiving this person as existing forever.

Sakti, which in Sanskrit means power, is related to the great Goddess and Mother of the universe, Shakti-Maya. More than an example of female power, *sakti* is the realization of the radiance and beauty of divine love. In a concept akin to the tantric, Celtic Druid liturgy expresses this spiritual union of energies with the saying, "perfect love and perfect peace." Simply put, this means the perfect love of the Goddess combined with the perfect peace of the God into Oneness, which is again where female and male energies come together.

Kundalini stems from the sanskrit word *kundal,* which means "coil." Kundalini is a vital Shakti force that is compared to a coiled, resting, or sleeping serpent. The nature of kundalini movements are spiraling and serpentlike. Chakras are psychic centers, and the Muladhara Chakra (root chakra) is the seat of the coiled kundalini energy force. The kundalini spiritual energy lies dormant and is coiled three-and-one-half times around the "self-born" lingham (penis). This foundation chakra is the root of all growth, and awareness of the divinity of humankind. The unawakened Kundalini Shakti remains coiled, wrapped around the lingham with her tail in her mouth.

Kundalini is an aspect of the eternal, divine consciousness, the Great Goddess, Shakti. Kundalini is energy in kinetic and static form, and this is present in all that exists in manifested reality. All creatures act through the power of kundalini. In the phenomenal world there is kundalini power in and behind every action. The ultimate experience is when mind and kundalini meet, and the union between Shiva and Shakti takes place—and that is as good as it gets!

The seat of Shakti, called Kundalini Shakti, is the root chakra, and the seat of Shiva is the crown chakra. The union of the Shakti, the female principle, and Shiva, the male principle, forms the basis of tantra. Kundalini Shakti sleeps coiled in the root chakra. To awaken kundalini from her slumber, you follow the Noble Eightfold Path of Buddha, purify your body through diet and meditation, and work with sound and visualization. When kundalini awakens she flows upward, through the second, third, fourth, fifth, and sixth chakras, finally reaching the seventh (crown) chakra to unite with Shiva, the divine lord of love. This union opens the doors to infinite knowledge and experience.

After Kundalini Shakti unites with Crown Shiva, they stay in union for a period of time, and then Kundalini Shakti descends downward to the root chakra and re-coils. As she descends, the energies of all of the chakras are restored and revitalized.

The Noble Eightfold Path of Buddha

The main teachings of Buddha are the Four Noble Truths and the Middle Way, with its Eightfold Path. The Four Noble Truths are: 1. life is suffering; 2. the cause of suffering is selfish desires; 3. suffering can be stopped; 4. there is a method that can be used to stop suffering called the Middle Way.

The Middle Way consists of eight steps called the Noble Eightfold Path. To awaken kundalini and reach Nirvana, you need to first follow the steps of the Eightfold Path:

1. Right to Knowledge—The knowledge of the Four Noble Truths.
2. Right Aspiration—Clearly devoted to being on the path toward Enlightenment.
3. Right Speech—Clarity of what you say (making certain you say what you genuinely mean) and speaking kindly, without malice.
4. Right Behavior—Reflecting on your behavior and the reasons for it. Honoring the five basic laws of behavior: not to kill, steal, lie, drink intoxicants, or commit sexual offenses.

5. Right Livelihood—Selecting an occupation that keeps you on the path, that is, a path that promotes life and well-being rather than the accumulation of money and wealth.
6. Right Effort—Directing your will and curbing selfish passions and wants, and actively moving along the path toward Enlightenment.
7. Right Mindfulness—Continuing self-examination and expanding your awareness. Remember, you are the result of your thoughts.
8. Right Concentration—Encouraging and experiencing a state of bliss and Nirvana.

Kundalini and Breath

Your breathing pattern can be pulled into entrainment with your heart, especially when you are in a state of love. The first step in accessing kundalini energy is to concentrate on your breath passing into your heart. When your heart feels bright, radiant, peaceful, and calm, your breath naturally moves upward and charges and triggers your other chakras. This is the time for kundalini energy to be released, when the heart is open and connected.

Breath is a profoundly intimate form of communion with existence. When you inhale, you open yourself up to the flow of life energy, enabling the energy to nourish and vitalize you. The air being drawn into your lungs carries vital energy that circulates through the subtle energetic pathways of your body. Breath and spirit have the same root word, *spirare,* which means "to breathe." Inspiration is breathing in the divine spirit, while expiration means the exit of spirit.

Deep, full breathing leads to peace, calm, and good health, while shallow breathing leads to emotional, mental, and physical disturbances and ill health. To balance both hemispheres of your brain, use the following simple technique. Close your right nostril and then exhale for six counts, and then inhale for three counts.

Switch and close your left nostril and exhale for six counts. Inhale for three counts, and then switch to your right side. Do this for about five minutes. When you breathe in through the right nostril you are breathing in solar or sun energy, and when you breathe in through your left nostril you breathe in lunar or moon energy.

In this exercise, you are seeking an overall state of internal coherence in which your mind, body, and spirit are in sync. Have your partner do the same exercise, and then bring both of your energies into sync with one another. If you now move this into sexual energy, where your mind, body and spirit are in sync and one, you can continue running this energy until you both reach ecstasy and merge into the divine light.

Awakening Kundalini

You function perfectly well without ever awakening kundalini, but you limit your consciousness and experience. Kundalini supports life and consciousness while remaining coiled, but once awakened it can lead to superconsciousness and divine wisdom. This comes about because the sense-mind is transformed into pure mind, which is absorbed by the stream of consciousness flowing in the form of Kundalini Shakti. The mind then moves beyond all the contraries and polarities while realizing pure being.

Method 1: The Swirling Rainbow

Focus on your chakras, one at a time, starting at the first foundation chakra and moving upward toward your crown. Open up each of the chakra centers, sensing the area as a clockwise spinning wheel of energy growing stronger and brighter. Visualize the following vibrant colors filling your chakras: root—red, navel—orange, solar plexus—gold, heart—green, throat—blue, third eye—violet, crown—white. Join the wheels and colors together into one large swirling rainbow. Do this for five minutes every day and notice the change in your personal energy.

Method 2: Elemental Kundalini

This can be performed solo or by a couple, standing, sitting, and/or reclining, and takes about two hours. You will want to remove all clothing for this experience. Read over the guidelines and then gather together everything you will need, and don't forget the matches.

Each of your first five chakras correspond to elemental energies, as follows:

Root chakra: earth element
Second chakra: water element
Third chakra: fire element
Fourth chakra: air element
Fifth chakra: ether (Akasha), Spirit

This awakening process applies these five elemental correspondences using physical representations: a bowl of earth, a cup or chalice of water, a candleholder with candle, incense or smudge, and a sacred object or personal symbol. Before you begin, gather these items together and place them in front of you on a table, counter, the floor, or ground. Position the items around you within easy reach, and in the appropriate directional corners: North (earth), East (air), South (fire), and West (water). I strongly recommend purchasing a small compass to determine the four corners. Place the representation of Spirit in front of you or, when working with your lover, between you. Spend fifteen minutes on each chakra.

1. Begin by focusing on your first (root) chakra. Also called the Muladhara, this is the point where earth energy enters your body and is the seat of passion located at the base of your spine. Some say the root chakra is located at the center of the pubic bone. Concentrate your attention on your root chakra as you visualize and sense things that are related to the earth. Your bones, flesh, skin, and hair consist of the earth element. Now take a pinch

of clean earth from the bowl and rub it on your lower stomach. When working with your lover, take another bit and rub the earth on your lover's lower stomach. Allow your partner to reciprocate. Slowly let the earth run through your fingers as you feel its fine, grainy, yet smooth texture.

2. Move upward to your second (navel) chakra. Also called the Svadistthana, this is the chakra of identity, personality, and emotions. Focus on the water element and sense your feelings, emotions, moods, and the blood that courses through your body. Hold the cup of water, take a sip, and then have your beloved take a sip. Next, dip your fingers into the cup of water, applying the drops to your navel area and rubbing the moisture into your skin. When working with your lover, rub droplets of water on his or her navel area. Allow your lover to reciprocate. Set the cup back down.

3. Move onward to your third (solar plexus) chakra and the fire element. Also called the Manipura, this chakra influences willpower, expression, and adaptability to change. See and sense things related to fire and light, such as the sun, and gaze into the light in your lover's eyes. Light the candle and hold the candleholder firmly, waving it back and forth in front of your solar plexus area, about nine inches away from your skin. Feel the warmth of the flame, but be careful not to burn yourself. When working with your lover, wave the flame close to your partner's solar plexus and then allow time for her or him to reciprocate. Set the candle down in a safe place.

4. Move to the fourth (heart) chakra, reflecting on the element of air. Also called the Anahata, your heart chakra is the point where energies entwine, where passion and unconditional love meet. Focus on the rhythm of your breathing, the breeze as it touches your face, and the heat of your lover's breath. Light the incense or smudge and use the smoke to cleanse and soothe you. Bathe in the pungent smoke, while noticing the way it moves and the patterns it takes.

5. Move your awareness to your fifth (throat) chakra and the

element of Spirit. Also called the Vishuddhi, this is the chakra of psychic power and spiritual communication. While visualizing and sensing the divinity of all things, make an effort to connect with the spirit within and without. Take your sacred object or symbol and place it on or near your throat chakra. Breathe in the spiritual essence and the light you feel reflected in the object or symbol. When working with your lover, place the sacred object or symbol on their body and allow them to reciprocate.

6. Take a minute or two to connect your chakras and the elements in a harmonious way by weaving them together with a golden thread of light. See and sense everything inside and outside of you as being part of an infinite fabric of rainbow light. Breathe this light in until you feel completely energized. Apply this energy to lovemaking, a creative project, or something else you take pleasure in.

Method 3: Sun and Moon Kundalini

This method works best with a clear quartz crystal or similar gemstone. If you don't have a crystal or gemstone, use the palm of your right hand.

Lie down comfortably, with pillows under your head, lower back, and beneath your knees, and your feet and hands uncrossed. Close your eyes and center yourself by seeing and sensing a wave of warm blue water washing over you. Breathe deeply several times.

Place the crystal in your right hand and hold it over your root chakra while visualizing the color red. Breathe the color into this chakra for a minute or two. Using the crystal as a focal, see and sense the harmonic of colored light in each of your chakras being reflected from the crystal. Move your right hand, with the crystal, to your navel chakra and visualize the color orange for a couple of minutes. Proceed to your solar plexus and visualize gold, and then to your heart chakra, visualizing green, and onward up to your throat chakra, seeing and sensing blue for a minute or two. Finally move your hand with the crystal up to your third eye and hold it there for a couple of minutes, all the while visualizing and sensing the color violet, and then position your hand and crystal on the top of your head for a minute or two while visualizing bright white.

Set the crystal down next to you and sense your spinal kundalini channels moving through your body. Begin visualizing and sensing the smooth liquid silver light of the moon flowing into your tailbone area, up through your spine and chakras. Breathe deeply for a few minutes and allow the moonlight to travel all the way up through your crown chakra. Next, see and sense the smooth silver moonlight flowing into the bottoms of your feet, up your legs, thighs, and torso, into your arms and out your hands. Focus on the flowing moonlight for a few minutes, allowing the silver light to clear and wash away any blockages you may experience throughout the areas it travels.

Now sense and see a glowing sun warming and flowing into your tailbone area, up through your spine and chakras. Breathe deeply for a few minutes and allow the warm sunlight to travel up through your crown chakra. Take a few moments to fill your spine chakras with warm glowing sunlight. Now feel the golden rays of healing light flowing into the bottoms of your feet and inhale the warm sunlight up through the energy pathways in your legs, into your thighs, torso, over your shoulders and arms, and out your hands.

Practice breathing the moon and sun into and through your kundalini channels and leg, arm, and hand pathways daily, once in the morning and once at night, for an entire moon phase. Focus on the movement of energy from your root to your crown chakra and from your feet to your hands. Each time you practice this method, make an effort to build the moon and sun energy a little brighter, enriching the energy centers in your body and fine-tuning your kundalini power.

Kundalini and Sex

Once you and your partner become in tune with your senses and chakras, you open your perceptions of the world. A simple touch can become an energetic connection between two intimate souls. Sex is an experience that happens on many levels, including the physical, mental, and spiritual. When you enhance the alignment of your physical, mental, and spiritual selves, then sexual experience and union moves much more energy.

In Indian folklore, the symbol of the lingam is associated with the Indian God Shiva and the crown chakra. More than just a phallic symbol, the lingham symbolizes the male creative energy of the God and thus the generative force of the universe. According to the *Kama Sutra* (see Bibliography), the classic Hindu treatise on love and sex, men are divided into three groups depending upon the size of their lingham. The three divisions are the hare man, the bull man, and the horse man.

At the other pole, the yoni is the symbol of female creative energy and the Goddess, Devi, or Mahadevi, associated with the root chakra. Together, Shiva and Devi convey the concepts of the procreation of the world, the divine parents, the principle of division into opposites, and reunion into harmony. In the *Kama Sutra,* women are divided into three groups depending upon the size of their yoni: a doe, a mare, or a female elephant.

Raising your kundalini through sex is obviously one of the fastest ways to connect with the divine. The *Kama Sutra* describes nine forms of union according to dimensions, with the horse man and mare, and bull man and doe woman forming a high union, while the horse man and doe woman form the highest union. The hare man and female elephant make the lowest union. The nine forms of union according to dimensions are as follows:

Equal Unions

(Equal unions are the best)

Women	Men
Deer	Hare
Mare	Bull
Elephant	Horse

Unequal Unions

(The highest and lowest unions are the worst, while the
high unions are better than the low unions.)

Women	Men	
Deer	Bull	High Union
Mare	Horse	High Union
Mare	Hare	Low Union
Elephant	Bull	Low Union
Elephant	Hare	Lowest Union
Deer	Horse	Highest Union

In other words, the closer the fit, the higher the union.

If you and your partner do the outlined kundalini methods
together, you establish a connection that reaches to the divine.
Combining this energy, you can transfer it into the sexual experience and toward creating positive patterns. Touch each other's
chakras and arouse each sense individually, building the sexual
experience to new heights. Ways of intensifying and expanding
your sexual experiences include using essential oils in almond, or
olive oil, and giving your lover a sensual massage, or in your bath,
or by placing a drop of oil on lightbulbs. You can also rub scented
oils, such as amber, rose, and lavender, on candles. The aroma fills
the room when you light the candles.

Burning incense also enhances your sexual experience. My

favorite sex-enhancing incenses are hand-rolled Tibetan incense, amber, and sandalwood incenses. Using charcoal in a large fireproof incense burner and then adding dried herbs, resins, and flowers such as lavender, copal, and sage is the most fun because of the variety and originality of the mixtures. Experiment with different types of incenses and select the ones that you and your partner prefer. If you use the same or similar scented incense every time you make love, you will find its scent triggers sensual memories and responses.

Touch is essential to almost all sexual experiences. Using patterns of touch can be very effective in sensual and sexual encounters. For example, you could trace rune symbols across your lover's body in a specific sequence. This would activate the energies of the runes, which can be used in sex magick.

Foods can also be used to enhance and heighten sexual experiences. Honey, whipped cream, and mint are all contemporary sex foods. Many massage oils come in different flavors, or you can make your own flavored massage oil using olive or almond oil mixed with a few drops of pure vanilla.

Music always adds to sexual experience. Play your favorite tunes, or mood music such as contemporary instrumental music, Celtic music, or any music that helps you relax and feel sensual and sexual. Also, playing music and singing together brings partners closer together. And almost everyone loves having a song written for them. By using essential oils, scents, touch, taste, and music, you can raise the level of energy, and sex becomes a divine experience.

4

Deepening Your Sexual Relationship

We quench our thirst
in an ancient ritual
drinking it all in
creating universes
from the perfect union
of contraction and bliss.
—Sirona Knight

An ancient tradition with near pornographic overtones comes from the Chinese Ming dynasty and involves keeping silk depictions of men and women engaged in making love. Sometimes drawn and painted very realistically, these pictures were used traditionally as a form of insurance with the Thunder God, who would not strike a house where intercourse was happening because that is when the yin and yang, or female and male forces, are in powerful flow. Since the couple cannot be making love twenty-four hours a day, they keep the pictures.

Using various physical and spiritual techniques to heighten and deepen the sexual experience has been a preoccupation since the beginning of humankind. Foreplay and after play are as important as the sexual experience itself. Philosophies like tantra have spent thousands of years cultivating sexual nuances until they rival a fine art, in which attention is paid to every detail. The result is an experience beyond mere description only because there are no words that come close to describing it.

Spiritual Sex

Spiritual sex and the practice of tantra focuses on the concept of cherishing your partner and deepening your sexual experience through touch and intimacy. By expanding the way you express yourself sexually to your partner, you add depth to your relationship. One of the main components to expanding yourself sexually is by being creative in your approach. This means being open to trying different things and increasing the sexual and spiritual bond between you and your beloved. The *Kama Sutra,* the classical Indian text on eroticism, describes twenty different kinds of kisses, for example, the throbbing, touching, straight, bent, or pressed kiss. (*Kama sutra* means "to sow love.")

Both sexuality and spirituality are a blend of polarities. Like rivers of energy, they emanate from the same source: Oneness. The poles of passion and withholding, intimacy and detachment, surrender and possession, often heighten erotic tension.

Allowing yourself to step into the mystery that is sexuality and spirituality is the first step to deepening your sexual relationship. When you combine the sexual with the spiritual, the experience takes on an added element, reaching across dimensions. The intimacy between yourself and your partner enhances both the spiritual and sexual aspects of your relationship.

Love is what brings joy in living, and sex is probably the most powerful dynamic at work in all of life. Together these energies can lead you to sacred and mystical states of consciousness and ecstacy. Expanding your capacity for having joy, love, and passion in your life creates truly satisfying relationships and a fulfilling sex life, which in turn helps you stay in touch with the magick and mystery of life.

A sexually healthy person is someone who experiences their body as a pleasurable place to be and who can receive touch and enjoy it. They know what touch they like and what they don't like, and can communicate their feelings and emotions clearly and effortlessly. They find the act of making love pleasurable and satisfying a good deal of the time, and inspiring and moving most of the time.

To be sexually healthy you need to be able to be honest about whether or not you are enjoying a fulfilling sex life, know how to sustain a positive relationship, and also enjoy your solitude and the time you spend alone. You know how to transform your sexual energy into manifesting patterns and any creative act you desire.

Upon accepting and embracing your sexual nature, you free its awesome power to use for your benefit. You no longer worship it or deny it, but instead come into balance and view your sexuality as part of your divinity. It becomes joyful, light, and loving. You learn to use sex for more than procreation, recreation, or physical gratification. Sex is creative energy. Magick is the art of creating reality, and true magick is simply the art of creating exactly what you want.

Some spiritual traditions, such as tantra, recognize the link between the spiritual and sexual. Part of this connection from spiritual to sexual again comes back to this idea of balancing polarities, and in the process optimizing and deepening your sexual experience to divine proportions.

Tantra

Tantra influences much of Eastern spiritual thought. The word *tantra* means "transformation of energy," and the tantric teachings focus on the transformation of vital energy. Tantra is simultaneously an Oriental philosophy, an artistic discipline, and a spiritual practice. Rooted in the mysteries of the Great Goddess, tantra uses the highest mystical teachings to access the power for transmission.

Realizing the unity of the body and spirit, of the human and the divine, is what tantra is all about. Tantra yoga comes from the Hindu yoga tradition that dates back thousands of years. When Shiva is united with Shakti, he has the power to create. Tantrika is a rich spiritual tradition of the Indian subcontinent whose literature dates back to the tenth century and whose adepts know the powerful secrets of sex.

Tantra describes how to harness and utilize the creative life force energy in sexuality to achieve states of higher consciousness. *Tantra* means "to weave or combine into union." Tantra weaves the seemingly opposite expressions of life force energy—male and female, active and receptive, yang and yin—into ecstatic union and bliss.

In Indian mythology, Shiva is a god of reproduction whose symbol is the lingham. One story tells of how Vishnu and Brahma encountered each other in the primeval universe and argued as to which of them was the progenitor of all beings. As they argued, a large fiery lingham rose up and grew into infinite space. Vainly, they both sought to measure it. Brahma, as the gander, flew up, and Vishnu, as the boar, dove down. Finally, the side of the giant phallus burst open, revealing Shiva within, who proclaimed himself the origin of the two while Vishnu and Brahma bowed before him.

In sacred sexuality the lingham is respectfully viewed and honored as a wand of light that channels creative energy and pleasure. It is the sanskrit word for the male sexual organ. *Yoni* is the sanskrit word for the vagina, which is loosely translated as "sacred space" or "sacred temple." The yoni is seen from a perspective of love and respect.

Accounts from Tibet regarding Tibetan tantra in the early twentieth century indicate that young tantra apprentices, both men and women, were treated as hermits. They dwelled in isolated caves and had their food brought to them twice a day, along with a sexual tantra teacher who came to them at intervals. They were to meditate upon sexual union with the teacher while she or he was away. Eventually these apprentices achieved a state of protracted sexual union with the absence of any physical entity. The lover, in her or his spiritual guise, not a physical one, was called a *tulpa*.

Treating your spiritual partner as a marvel, as someone to be delighted in, to be cherished, is a major thrust of tantra. Spirited living adds magic and relish to everyday acts. In tantra, the term *sakti* in Sanskrit means "power," and is related to the great Goddess and Mother of the universe, Shakti-Maya. It describes the moment when female and male energies come together as one.

The essence of tantra is an experience of moving beyond space and time, of surpassing the seeming duality of reality and of recovering the primordial unity. In tantra you come to know and honor the energies of God and Goddess and the manifested and unmanifested aspects of Oneness.

Having the experience of touch and profound contact with things, other people, and the universe is the primary focus of tantra. The less mental interference and analytical thought you have, the better. In tantric practice, the thirty-six *tattvas*, or universal categories, activate through touch.

Tattva translates as "the Truth of Brahman." The thirty-six *tattvas* are:

The five elements: earth, water, fire, air, and space.
The five impressions: scent, taste, sight, touch, and hearing.
The instruments of action: excreting, sexing, grasping, moving, speaking.

The instruments of sensing: smelling, tasting, seeing, feeling, and
hearing.
The empirical individual: Prakriti, Ahamkara, Buddhi, Manas,
and Purusha.
Limitation of Maya: action, knowing, desire, time, and fate.
The five verities: Kriya, Jnana, Iccha, Shakti, and Shiva.
The thirty-sixth *tattva* is Shiva-Shakti

In tantra, you activate and experience the *tattvas* in preparation
for sacred sex.

The Great Union of Shiva and Shakti manifests in the upper
brain center, known as Sahasrara. The Sahasrara Chakra, at the
crown of the head, is also called the thousand-petalled lotus.

In the Great Union ritual, Shiva adores Shakti, and their passion
traverses all states, which moves through all the thirty-six *tattvas*. In
other words, this union stretches from the earthly *tantrika* tasting the
Goddess to her divine absorption into Shiva. All these stages live in
the most intense and complete manner, in which all human passions
and desires are satisfied during the energetic ascent toward union.

In tantric practice there is a subtle building of a charge of
energy in the body. This powerful energy is drawn upward to your
higher energy centers with conscious intention, using creative
visualization, which unites you with your beloved as well as the
divine spirit. In tantric lovemaking, you and your lover synchronize your breathing and circulate your sexual energy through your
hearts. You connect your heart with your genitals, which creates a
natural coherence and an experience of Oneness. Sex becomes a
meaningful, energetic, and spiritual way of communicating—with
each other, and ultimately with the divine Spirit.

For most couples, the three main things that are most helpful in
tantra are: 1. For men to avoid ejaculating each time they have
sex so they can increase their vital energy; 2. for lovers to breathe
together and move their energy as one; 3. to see making love as a
spiritual or meditative experience instead of being goal-related or
as some sort of "performance."

Neo-Tantra

Tantra is the word most used to describe sacred sex. The form of tantra practiced by Western culture is actually neo-tantra, which is a collection of esoteric traditions that include Eastern tantra, Native American, Pagan, Mesoamerican, and Hindu.

Neo-tantra, as practiced in Western cultures such as the United States, is a fresh eclectic blend of sacred and New Age philosophies and practices drawn from ancient and modern esoteric traditions around the world. For instance, in neo-tantra it is common to see kundalini methods combined with sex magick techniques. In this way neo-tantra allows access to all divine realities of Gods and Goddesses, elementals, devas, faeries, spirit guides, ancestors, and so forth, no matter what your spiritual path. In neo-tantra you can channel archetypal energies such as Kama, the Hindu love God, or Venus, the Roman love Goddess, and use those energies to drive your creation or affirmation.

Tantra Practice for One

For one day, or part of a day, treat yourself as the most important person in your life by indulging in some of your favorite things. For example, get out of the house and go to a concert, a movie you've been wanting to see, to a baseball game, Renaissance Faire, or other special event. Take yourself out to dinner at a lavish black-tie restaurant, on a picnic to the beach, or to a favorite place in nature. Indulge (within reason) your every desire for a few hours.

As the day concludes and you return home, put on some romantic music. Soft piano, guitar, harp, or flute music is a good choice, as is soft jazz, country, classical, and other New Age instrumental and vocal selections. The important thing is that the music is pleasing to you. I encourage you to try different types of music, including Eastern music, which is a natural choice and adds to the ambiance and mood of this tantric practice. If you are a musician, you may want to play your own compositions for a while as a way to unwind before putting on a musical selection.

Be sure to turn your phone machine on and turn the volume off, or unplug the phone. Make every effort to secure your privacy for this experience and make certain you will not be interrupted for a couple of hours.

Place representations of the four elements—earth, air, fire, and water—in each of the four corners of your tantric space, together with fresh flowers, crystals, and gemstones. All types of flowers will enhance this experience, especially fragrant ones such as roses, lavender, violets, geraniums, hyacinths, and orchids. Clear quartz crystals, rose quartz, or rutile quartz placed close by your bed, on your altar, or in the corners of your room will amplify the energy of your experience. If using crystal points be sure to point them toward your bed. Please refer to the Source Directory for a listing of places from which to obtain crystals and gemstones.

You may want to set up a tantric altar, covering it with a red altar cloth and adding focals such as incense, herbs, flowers, and symbols. Representations of the Goddess and God, yoni and ling-ham, can be placed on your altar. Be creative and leave the altar set up for at least three days.

Take a long sensuous bath, scenting the water with a few drops of rose or lavender oil. Then try a self-massage with vanilla, jasmine, lemon, or orange oil. You can also place a drop of essential oil on the lightbulbs in your tantric space. When the lights are switched on, the heat of the bulb will release the scent into the room.

When choosing focals use tantric colors: red for lust and sex; white, pink, and lavender for friendship and spiritual love; rose for sensual love; and green for growing love and fertility. For example, dress in red lingerie or drape a large red scarf or red cotton towel around you. Lower or turn off the lights in your tantric space and light candles to create a more romantic and mysterious ambience. Choose red, white, purple, and pink taper and votive candles, and anoint them with essential lavender and rose oils before lighting them.

Finish your experience with an intimate evening of solo sexual ecstasy. If you are in a relationship, suggest that your partner try the Tantra for One practice within the next week. Within the next couple of weeks, try the Tantra for Two practice.

Tantra Practice for Lovers

Doing this powerful Tantra Practice for Lovers with your sexual partner transforms your concepts of love and sex. You will want a private and quiet setting, and at least two hours when you know you will not be disturbed. Always practice safe sex and be honest with yourself and your partner about your intentions and expectations. Read this section completely before you enter into this experience. Certain preparations will need to be made beforehand, such as gathering supplies and having them on hand.

In your bedroom, burn jasmine, sandalwood, vanilla, rose, or patchouli incense or herbs over charcoal. Lower the lights and make sure your space is as comfortable as possible. Rub essential oil of rose or lavender on taper and votive candles to create a romantic setting.

Place fresh flowers in the room, choosing red, pink, lavender, and white blossoms. Sprinkle a few flower petals on your bed to add the beauty of nature to your experience. Consider setting up a special altar in the north or east corner, or the center of your bedroom. On it place images of the Goddess and God, incense, herbs, magickal symbols and tools, fresh flowers, stones, and other items you feel appropriate to the occasion. (Please refer to the appendices.)

Begin by feeding each other love foods that heighten sensitivity, such as apples, apricots, dates, brazil nuts, ginger, licorice, raspberries, strawberries, endive salads, olives, and chocolates. Also drink mint, hibiscus, and camomile teas.

Draw a deep warm bath, not too hot, and bathe with your lover by candlelight. Be sure to add a few drops of rose, lavender, ylang-ylang, or geranium oil. You can also rub a drop of essential oil on your pillowcases and sheets. If you prefer a shower to a bath, use scented soaps such as lavender or rose. Dress each other in red, rose, or white, and then slowly undress each other or undress for each other, whichever you prefer.

Put on some soft music and meditate or sit quietly together by candlelight, all the while looking directly into each other's eyes. Do this for about five to ten minutes. Match each other's breathing patterns until it is as if you are breathing as one.

Next, use a votive candle in a sturdy holder to study your lover's face, eyes, hair, neck, chest, torso, arms, and legs, shining the candlelight slowly across her or his body. Be careful not to drip wax on sensitive skin, hair, fabrics, or the rug.

Follow with a sensual massage, perfuming each other with the scented massage oil. In the traditional technique, anoint your lover with oil, starting with the heart, then behind each ear, the wrists, ankles, and the back of the head. Continue with a sensual massage, softly rubbing and caressing your partner's back, arms, legs, face, and feet, and then moving your hands to more intimate areas. Embrace or touch for at least fifteen minutes before sexual intercourse. Unite your breathing in long and deep rhythmic breaths. Let go of all tensions, worries, concerns, self-conscious doubts, and fears that may enter your awareness. Surrender completely to the love and light in your lover's eyes. Allow that light to guide you and keep you moving toward feelings of love. Sense the mystery in your lover's eyes as if you have always known each other, that deeper connection that is unexplainable and unfathomable.

See your lover as a face of the divine, as a divine being, and as a body of light and love. You may have a "spiritual or sacred experience" at this point. Just register it, and continue to focus on the love you feel and the light in your lover's eyes.

Make love by candlelight, making an effort, once again, to match your breathing patterns. As you are making love, be completely still for a few minutes, and gaze deeply into your lover's eyes, sensing the love you feel for your partner. Slowly, sacredly, bring each other to the height of desire and ecstatic delight, like the Goddess and God awakening their senses. This is a time for recognizing yourselves as a divine couple, like Shakti and Shiva, Isis and Osiris, Dagda and Morrigan. Totally abandon yourself to each other in this most sacred encounter.

Ways to Enhance Your Tantra Experience

- Sleep naked and try sleeping on different sides of the bed on alternate nights.

- Draw a sacred circle of light or other sacred geometric figure, either energetically or physically, around the perimeter of your tantric area.

- Chant the mantra OM together while making love.

- Create a symbol of your tantra experience by drawing a picture, composing a song or poem, or planting a patch of flowers, a special love pot, or a windowbox of poppies, tulips, miniature roses, lavender, or daisies.

- Use the art of feng shui to create a harmonic living and loving space in your bedroom and home.

Bedroom Feng Shui

The feng shui of any environment, indoors and outdoors, can be ascertained using the Ba-Gua. The Ba-Gua is a octagonal grid or map based on the symbols of the I Ching, the ancient oracle that feng shui is based on. The Ba-Gua grid, or overlay, is placed over land, cities, neighborhoods, as well as structures, rooms within a house, decks, and beds to show where there are missing spaces or negative energies that need rectifying or curing.

The sacred art of placement called feng shui enhances your living space, just as tantra and neo-tantra enrich your sexual experience. Feng shui, like magick, works off the principle of homeopathic magick, which describes inanimate objects, as well as plants and animals, as being able to diffuse blessing or bane around them, according to their own intrinsic nature. It is the skill of the practitioner or feng shui master to either tap into or block this stream of positive or negative energy.

Feng shui masters learned their art from the Gods, and today this four thousand-year-old Eastern tradition is experiencing a rebirth in the New Age theater. *Feng shui* refers to "the way of the wind and water," working with the flow of natural forces of energy. Feng shui practitioners follow the premise that everything is made of energy, or *chi,* and everything emits energy fields that either help or harm your personal energy field. Cutting fields of energy, called *sha,* can be neutralized and transformed by using various cures.

The chi flow in your bedroom needs to be soft and enriching, because this is where you spend your time regenerating your body through rest and deepening your sacred relationships through touch and sex. If your bedroom is too close to the entryway of your home, you may never feel really rested. Make an effort to orient your bed slightly away from the wall or, better yet, in the middle of the room and off the floor, so the chi energy can flow all around you. Chi energy may flow out of your body if your feet are pointed toward the door of your bedroom. A simple cure for this position is to hang a crystal overhead between the door of the bedroom and your feet. To find out how the chi flows in your bedroom, light incense or smudge and watch the way the smoke moves.

Working in harmony with the elements and creating positive change in your bedroom is what bedroom feng shui is all about. Using the eight-sided energetic overlay called the Ba-Gua, which is based on the energetics of the eight directions, Chinese I Ching trigrams, and the location of your front door, you can tune and transform the energies of your bedroom or any room of your house. Each person's interpretation of the Ba-Gua is unique in that everyone's concepts, likes, and dislikes are different. The eight sides of the Ba-Gua are career, knowledge, family/health, wealth, fame, marriage, children/creativity, and helpful people/travel. For instructions for specific Ba-Gua bedroom layouts, please refer to Appendix F.

Suggestions for the marriage area of your bedroom Ba-Gua are to place mementos from your handfasting and/or marriage in this area, along with handfasting and wedding pictures. The marriage box (see Chapter 6) is also placed in this location. Put marriage-related items or gifts on a table in the marriage corner and fill a vase with beautiful white, pink, red flowers (real or silk). The peony, chrysanthemum, lotus, white magnolia, and the orchid are the five flowers traditionally considered most beneficial for feng shui. The peony symbolizes love and honor, and, when it flowers, good fortune and wealth. Try hanging a potted plant in the marriage corner to keep your marriage growing, or a wind chime to move your relationship into a higher consciousness. Drape a chair, four-poster bed, or bench with red, pink, or white lace or velvet and use the same color of silk or satin sheets.

Power animals and totems serve as guardians in our homes, both protecting and bringing their special qualities into the living space. (Examples of power animals and totems are the wolf, bear, eagle, and raven. Power animals are often animals that you have a special connection with, and can be of any size. They sometimes appear in your dreams or may be animals you have always felt an affinity with, such as cats, dogs, or birds. Totems are considered to be ancestors, friends, and protectors of humankind.) You can bring this power into your bedroom by placing a painting, statue, or picture of the animal in a place of prominence, depending upon where you want to integrate the animal energies. For example, you could use a representation of power animals such as the hawk and wolf, two animals that mate for life.

When the energy needs to be harmonized because of a sharp corner, a missing corner of a room, or other unbalanced spacial configuration, feng shui cures are used. These include crystals and gemstones that disperse, pull, push, and scatter energy. When chi energy encounters a crystal ball, cluster, or obelisk, the energy hits the object and diffuses in several directions, much like the way light moves through a prism. Crystal spheres or balls placed in windows send healing chi energy throughout the room. A faceted crystal ball captures the harsh sha energy and the facets break up the sha into chi. Faceted lead crystal balls in all sizes, which are used specifically for feng shui, are available from most New Age and metaphysical stores.

Other feng shui cures are heavy objects, such as carved statues of stone, wood, or metal, and large plants. The wayward and flighty impulses of love are counteracted by the weight of a heavy stone, the steadying influence of rose quartz, jade, or granite placed in the marriage corner of your bedroom. A large living or silk plant would have a similar effect, adding the element of growth to the marriage corner.

Moving objects such as wind chimes and mobiles create positive chi, as do animals and fish tanks. Be sure your windchimes are made of hollow rods rather than solid ones to allow the chi energy to flow upward. Tabletop water fountains and fish tanks are often placed in the wealth position of the Ba-Gua. Fish tanks customarily have eight goldfish for prosperity and one black fish for protection.

Electronic appliances such as televisions, lamps, telephones, and alarm clocks create energy fields and effect the chi energy in your bedroom. Suggestions would be to position your television in the knowledge corner of your bedroom and your phone in the helpful-people corner. If your work centers around the phone or television, you could place these appliances in the career, fame, or wealth positions in your bedroom's Ba-Gua.

Bells, red ribbons, silk flowers, bamboo flutes, and mirrors, probably the most widely used, also serve as feng shui cures. The traditional feng shui mirror is eight-sided. Mirrors are used to reflect energy back, for example, positive chi from a picture window. Use your intuition and be creative when selecting items for your bedroom.

In addition to the physical modifications of feng shui, ritual is used to lock the energies of your bedroom in place. You reinforce cures by adding the transcendental solution through ritual. Feng shui ritual uses the Three Secrets Reinforcement, which combines: 1. mudra, placing your left hand over the right hand and joining your thumbs at a forty-five degree angle; 2. mantra, which is saying OM, MA, NI, PAD, ME, HUM, repeated nine times in each of the corners and center of the Ba-Gua; and 3. creative visualization, which is where you visualize and sense what you wish to happen. I recommend you reinforce your Ba-Gua patterns as often as possible with the Three Secrets Reinforcement until you feel that every part of yourself and your space is in agreement and alignment with your intentions.

Feng shui can help create a harmonious and balanced environment in your bedroom and throughout your home. This energetic harmony and balance improves your health, clarity of mind, awareness, and alertness. Because of this you have the energy and wisdom to deal with daily life. A list of basic feng shui cures follows:

The Nine Basic Cures of Contemporary Feng Shui

1. Bright, shiny, light-refracting objects
2. Sounds
3. Living objects
4. Moving objects
5. Heavy objects
6. Electrical objects
7. Bamboo flutes
8. Colors
9. Miscellaneous

The Remedies of Traditional Feng Shui

The Five Activities/Phases/Elements—earth, metal, water, wood, and fire.

PART III

⤬

MAGICK

M agick is the art and practice of using energy to influence and alter events on the physical, mental, and
spiritual planes. Rather than being rigid and solid,
physical matter is fluid and made up of energy, and radiates an
energetic field that comes into contact and connects with other
energetic fields. Magick happens when the physical, mental, and
spiritual planes connect together as one, facilitating the movement of energy from one plane to another.

Sexual experience generates great amounts of energy on its
own, but when combined with magick becomes a potent force
and abundant source of energy for the fruition of your patterns. Sex, like magick, touches the physical, mental, and spiritual planes, which again releases energy through all three planes,
particularly when you use intention, expectation, desire, and
merging to amplify and direct the energy.

Sex magick builds even more energy when you use ritual
along with sexual and spiritual union with your lover. By doing
so, you can use this divine and light-filled energy to increase
your awareness and intimacy with yourself, your partner, and
the world. The basic idea behind magickal ritual is to provide a
guide or template for achieving higher states of consciousness
through your connection to the divine energy in whatever
form and way you wish to perceive it.

Chapters 5 and 6 give information, techniques, and rituals
for using sex and magick to enhance your life. Chapter 5 talks
about how to put together magickal patterns and how to use
ritual to create these patterns in reality. Chapter 6 gives no-
nonsense guidelines and rituals for achieving sacred and divine

love, sex, and magick within your relationship. By using magickal focals such as candles, essential oils, and ritual, you
heighten your awareness, adding spice and magick to your life
and your relationship. So, get ready for a sexual and spiritual
journey with definite erotic and magickal overtones. Remember to always practice safe sex, as sexual experience should be a
joyful and empowering act.

5

Magickal Patterning and Ritual

However far we travel
Wherever we may roam
The center of the circle
Will always be our home,
The gods are in the heavens
The angels treat us well
The oracle has spoken
We cast the perfect spell.

—John Lennon

Every relationship is essentially a pattern comprising the combined energies of each partner. The exchange of energy between two people has a pattern to it, from day-to-day interaction to higher exchange on a spiritual and energetic level. As a pattern, a relationship is what the two people make it, and optimally each person gives energy to the relationship and in turn gets what they need from it. To make the pattern of the relationship magickal involves raising its overall harmonic using love, sex, and magick.

Tapping Into the Source

The experiences of love, sex, and magick all tap into the source of creation and result in a surge of energy. This surge is akin to having a wave of energy break across your physical, mental, and spiritual realities. As this process unfolds, normal boundaries of time and space become blurred within the experience. An example of this is when you are with someone you love and time seems to blur. Time often seems to pass quickly while at the same time moving slowly, which again points to the meeting of polarities on multilevels within the experiences of love and sex.

A magickal pattern or relationship is what happens when you take love and sex and tap into its source, giving the experience divine and spiritual qualities. Like herbs, magick is the spice of life, and it turns a relationship into a feast of sensual pleasures. Attaining a magickal state of consciousness in your relationship heightens the senses and perceptions of yourself and your lover.

William Blake said, "If the doors of perception were cleansed, everything would appear to man as it is, infinite." Within this statement there exist three basic concepts. First, there is the idea of perception, which is the primary step in turning the raw data of the universe into some semblance of reality. Second, the doors allude to your senses, which are your means of perceiving your world. According to researchers on perception, humans with intact nervous systems have as many as seventeen senses. The more senses you use and the clearer and more fine-tuned they are, the more depth your perceptions and experiences will have. Third, William Blake's statement ties sensory perception to the infinite and divine quality of the universe. It says that if your senses and perception were completely clear of any distortion, your sensory perception would be a direct link to a spiritual and divine experience of infinite quality.

Far from being passive, your perception of the world is colored by your own unique set of experiences. The melding of yourself with the outside world is what makes the doors of perception magickal. Just by clearing your senses and listening, looking, smelling, tasting, and feeling, you turn what is around you into your world.

The movement of sensory perception is two-way in that images move inward but also outward. A glance contains the characteristics of a carrier wave, transmitting mental intention toward the object being viewed. This also holds true for the other senses that make up your perception of the world, and is consistent with the ideas of Aristotle and the ancient world that that perception confers reality. On one hand, perception floods in to create your reality, but on the other hand, awareness is moving outward to create your perceptions. At this point the process is circular, with perception acting as the dynamic force in the whole process.

The Magickal Reality

Experiences of the higher self have no guidelines of normalcy. Within modern society, each person rows toward a beacon of light that guides them across the dark waters. Within a relationship, you couple with another person on this journey of the spirit. Once you chart your course, you set a pattern that moves you from one perception to another.

In the realm of magick, earthly realities become part of the transient moment. Moving from the future into the now, in the present moment events are first left behind, and then disposed of and buried in the past. Within this now, which is both transient and eternal, the mind is prepared to accept the incredible, which is a world where different laws apply. In this world you are relieved of all the binds that tie you down, making you free, unfettered, and divine.

On a subtle level, the Indian Rishis believe everything is light and that light is the finest level of appearance before creation dissolves into pure consciousness. On this level, everything is reduced to patterns of light, which can be read and influenced by perception. The ability to sense and effect light at this level is very important and plays heavily into what is termed magick.

On a scientific level, quantum physicists have reduced everything down into terms of energy, of which light is a component. As with the Rishis' concepts of light, energy in a quantum sense is both observed and influenced. This scientifically validates the esoteric and magickal view that the observer has a definite impact on what is being observed through intention. This differs from the traditional view, which believed that scientists are impartial observers of the phenomena that take place around them.

One of the most important aspects of magick involves your ability to change your definition of a situation. Within this construct, changing the story in your mind induces changes within your attitudes and performances with regard to the situation. You change your inner realities by intentionally guiding your mental processes, i.e., directing your own experience. At this point your ideas and the energy of your thoughts have a profound impact on the world. The enormous power of your imagination is the fuel that guides your perceptions through reality. Thought is power and can wisely be used to enhance your life and manifest patterns. Through your intention, thoughts, actions, and merging, you can create the reality you desire.

Reading and Influencing Magickal Patterns

Part of cleansing your doors of perceptions involves learning to perceive your world without distortion. This is not an easy task, because as I mentioned in the section on intimacy, people are taught to build walls and boundaries around themselves. These have a tendency to dull the senses and, as a result, distort and skew perception.

Learning to be intimate with yourself and your partner is a way of cleansing perception. Once your senses become clear, you begin perceiving the connectedness of everything around you. Within these connections are the infinite patterns of energy and life. On a divine level, these are magickal patterns whose synchronicity unfolds like a blossoming flower.

Reading magickal patterns is a matter of cleanly perceiving the information coming in from your senses. Conversely, influencing magickal patterns is about the outward flow of perception and energy. This speaks to the natural unfolding of the mind's deeper layers. The philosophy of the Rishis encompasses the idea that within each person is the power to command every force of nature and to influence every atom in the universe.

Within Celtic Druid tradition is a technique for influencing patterns that involves using intention (expectation), desire, and merging. Called the Three Eyes of Kerridwen, intention, desire, and merging can be used to influence any pattern within your life.

Intention in cooking is the process of deciding what you want to make and eat. Desire is where you draw up the recipe for making what you want, and merging is the step where everything is blended together and cooked, if successful, into something that is consistent with your original intention.

In terms of relationships, an example would be that your intention is have a more fulfilling relationship with your partner, starting with lots more love, sex, and magick. The important thing is to be clear about your intention. Sometimes this may take some searching within yourself until you come up with a clear image of what you want. Intention is the cornerstone in influencing patterns, because a clear image of what you want going in has a profound effect on how things come out.

Desire is how much you want something to happen. You mentally and emotionally map the steps involved in getting what you have set your intention on. In the case of a deeper rapport with your mate, you need to go over the steps that would achieve this end. As you imagine each step, fill it with your desire for a successful outcome. Use all of your senses—see it, touch it, hear it, taste it, feel it, intuit it—until the image seems an innate part of yourself.

Once the image reaches this point, the time comes to merge with your intention and desire, triggering and manifesting the pattern. This means moving these mental images into physical reality while merging or becoming one with the divine. By becoming more aware of what love is and how it can be nourished you make your relationship into a loving and mutually beneficial exchange.

Sex is the driving force of a relationship because of the inherent polarities of male and female, linking back to the primal need within every living thing to have these polarities consummated and brought into balance. At this point, the connection and energies reach straight into the divine wholeness that connects us all.

Magick is the light that glows around something, making it special. By putting a little magick in your life you add a sparkle and zing that comes straight from the source. When someone says something is magickal, they mean it is wonderful, light-filled, and beyond normal reality. Putting that magick into your life is what reality and dreams are made of. Magick is that place where dreams and reality become one.

Magickal thinking exhibits many characteristics of what Rupert Sheldrake calls a morphogenic field. A perception suffused with awareness becomes profoundly intimate to a person in unity. Separations and boundaries break down as you perceive your relationship and connection to the whole of creation. The flow of perception inward and outward becomes one stream moving in and out. Within this moment, people are at their healthiest, and their lives are most in balance and in tune with the energies of the universe. It is also the best time to do magick.

To gain mastery over the ability to make your deepest desires come true, you must commit yourself to reaching a higher state of being. Fine-tune your senses—perform seasonal rituals, practice magickal patterning, connect with Oneness—until your perceptions are as infinite as the whole of existence. At this level, your life and relationship take on magickal qualities. Each experience connects into a larger one, moving into an even larger experience that eventually extends into divine infinity. By putting the images together you perceive the larger picture, which is the synchronicity that connects everything to the magickal pattern and wholeness of existence.

Best Days for Magick and Ritual

Ritual and magick are ways to tap into the creative and divine power of the universe. The techniques and magickal methods are derived from the Gwyddonic Druid Tradition, which is an ancient Welsh Druid Tradition. There are many other esoteric and magickal traditions, and I encourage you to synthesize their teachings as well, creating your own eclectic blend of magickal skills and rituals.

Magickal ritual consists of setting up an altar, drawing the sacred circle, and working with the elemental powers of nature, as well as healing works and gaining rapport with the Goddess and God. I must admit I prefer doing ritual with my husband and spiritual partner, but I employ the same basic methods when working as a couple, in a group, or solo.

The best time to perform rituals is on the Eight Great Days and the full moons. Following is a list of the days with the highest magickal power:

The Eight Great Days—Path of the Sun

1. Yule, Winter Solstice, or at 0 degrees Capricorn
2. Bridget's Fire, February 2, or at 15 degrees Aquarius
3. Hertha's Day, Spring Equinox, or at 0 degrees Aries
4. Beltane, May 1, or at 15 degrees Taurus
5. Letha's Day, Summer Solstice, or at 0 degrees Cancer
6. Lughnassad, first week of August, or at 15 degrees Leo
7. Hellith's Day, Autumn Equinox, or at 0 degrees Libra
8. Samhain, October 31, or at 15 degrees Scorpio

The Thirteen Moons—Path of the Moon

Begin with the first high moon after Yule.

1. Wolf Moon: unity, dormancy, and potential
2. Storm Moon: duality and polarity (as above, so below)
3. Chaste Moon: the threefold trinity of the Maiden, Mother, and Crone; and Son, Father, and Grandfather
4. Seed Moon: the foundation four elements of manifestation and utilizing elemental energies
5. Hare Moon: control of the self and physical reality
6. Dyad Moon: time and space shift, multidimensions, and boons
7. Mead Moon: lunar fertility, lucid dreams, and spiritual connection
8. Wort Moon: the yearly cycle; the beginning, middle, and end
9. Barley Moon: wisdom, knowledge, and skill
10. Wine Moon: prophecy and divination
11. Blood Moon: maternity, fecundity, and ancestral communication
12. Snow Moon: divine, royal, or noble purpose and intention
13. Oak Moon: the lunar cycle, rebirth, and transmigration

Note: The Oak Moon is not used in twelve full moon years.

Setting Up Your Altar

An altar enriches your spiritual life by offering a sacred space right at home where you can find peace, celebrate ritual, and ask for divine guidance and help. Approaching the altar, with its candles, incense, and magickal tools, instantly evokes feelings of self-empowerment, spirit, and mystery.

Set up your altar before you begin your magickal work or ritual. An altar can be made from just about anything: a carved antique table, chair, tree stump, or a cloth spread on the ground. It is customary to set up your altar in the North, East, or Center Point, depending on your preference. Make certain the surface is stable and safe to burn a candle on. The Goddess, or left side of the altar, holds the feminine nurturing elements of water and earth. The God, or right side of the altar, holds the power elements.

Optional ways of setting up your altar include dividing it into four or five quadrants and placing the ritual tools in the appropriate positions: the bowl of salt or earth in the North, the wand or incense in the East, the athame or sword in the South, and the chalice of water in the West. You can add images of power animals to your altar, such as the wolf (North), owl (East), salamander (South), and dolphin (West), thereby invoking the energies of these animal totems into your ritual and sacred space. Another option is dividing the altar into twelve quadrants, with each corresponding to a different sign of the zodiac.

Your altar design needs to be fluid, reflecting the changes of the seasons, the phases of the moon, and your hopes and desires. In the spring, daisies, daffodils, and tulips might dress your altar; in the winter, pine cones and pine or fir boughs can be placed on your sacred table. Each person using the altar customarily contributes something.

In the Gwyddonic Druid tradition, there are six Tools of the Art and Craft you will want to gather and use to make your magick more powerful and potent. Each of these six tools, as well as their contents, represent each of the elements, as follows:

Tool	*Element*
Bowl	Earth
Wand	Air
Athame	Fire
Chalice	Water
Incense holder	Air
Candleholder (white candle)	Fire

Optional Altar Items

> Red or green altar cloth
> Two additional candleholders and sticks (one red and one
>   green, representing the God and Goddess) to be used on the
>   altar
> Additional cup or chalice for wine or juice to be used on the
>   altar
> Journal to write ritual experiences in
> A nine-foot-long cord
> A Ritual robe or tunic

Used for triggering whole-brain activity, your tools are imbued with the sacred energies of the Goddess and God, and are energetically alive. Examine the energies of the tools you select and clear all unwanted energies by smudging, passing them carefully through the flame of a sacred fire, washing them in salt water, or setting them out in the sunlight or moonlight.

Prepare your magickal ritual area by taking a bowl of water and putting some sea salt in it. Then take a sprig of greenery and dip it in the salt water. Sprinkle your altar and ritual area in a clockwise (sunwise) pattern as you say, "Begone from here all darkness and foulness. Begone from this place in Our Lady's Name!" Repeat this a total of three times. While you are sprinkling the salt water around your ritual area, simultaneously visualize a cobalt blue light washing out the area energetically.

Set your altar table with everything you will need for the magickal work, and if you are using invocations or chants, place them where you can reach or read them easily.

Step-by-step instructions for drawing a sacred circle or for calling in the wards, presented later in this chapter, are examples of invocations and chants you may want to have handy. When doing other types of magick, such as candle love magick, you may want to write down a specific chant, such as "Divine light burning bright, bring true and lasting love to me tonight," or "Bridget, Bridget, Bridget, sacred flame, Oh Shining One, bring my true love to me, riding on the rays of the morning sun." Chants and invocations can be those you find in books, on the Internet, learn from others, or original ones that you pen yourself.

Put the objects that represent the Goddess and God in a prominent position on the altar so that your invocations and gestures may be made before them and in their direction. Be sure to light all candles and incense before you begin your magickal ritual and extinguish them once you are finished. Traditionally, the candles are allowed to burn all the way down. After you perform your work, clap your hands soundly three times and then purify yourself, for example, by taking a salt bath, a short walk, or drinking a large glass of water. Be sure to put everything away when you are done.

Consecrating Altar Objects

Consecrate your own tools by merging deeply with the divine energies of the Goddess and God, with the intention of imbuing the tools with the elemental qualities they embody. Make your altar items magickal by merging and becoming one with the Goddess or God and then imparting their divine energy and aspects into the object you are focusing on. Visualize and sense the power of the Goddess and God, and then use your breath to physically pulse the divine energy into the item by breathing in and sharply exhaling through your nose. Do this at least three times, and for better results, nine times. Your breath and focused intention are the carrier waves that transport and imbed divine energy into the object.

Some say that if you wash your altar tools with dew before sunrise on May Day (Beltane) morning, the day of lovers, it fills them with divine power and knowledge, which you can use to create a successful and sacred relationship. As well as using dew to consecrate your tools, you can also use the four elements—earth, air, fire, and water—to charge your ritual tools and other items with powerful elemental energies.

Drawing the Sacred Circle

Cast your sacred circle of light by visualizing a brilliant blue-white flame flowing out of your outstretched palms and fingertips as you slowly and deliberately spin clockwise. Magickal tools such as the athame or wand are also customarily used to draw the sacred circle. When working with tools, visualize the blue-white flame flowing out of the tip of the tool.

The main purpose of the sacred circle is to create a protected and energetically positive magickal working space. The sacred circle is a vortex of light. Within the circle you achieve a higher awareness and tuning of body, mind, and spirit, creating a connection to the divine and Oneness.

Construct the circle as large or small as you desire or to fit your needs. For instance, if you are working indoors, you will want to cast the circle around a particular room or building, but when doing magickal works outdoors you may want to cast a sacred and protective circle around an entire meadow or mountain.

Standing at the North point (where your altar is positioned), take the sprig of greenery, dip it in the salt water, and wave it softly at the North point. Chant aloud, "Ayea, Ayea Kerridwen! Ayea, Ayea Kernunnos! Ayea, Ayea, Ayea!" After purifying the North point, continue on to the East, South, and West points respectively, sprinkling salt water at these corners and repeating the chant each time. When working with a partner, chant in unison. Feel free to be creative and compose your own chant. For example, "Ayea, Ayea Great Mother! Ayea, Ayea Great Father! Ayea, Ayea, Ayea!"

Next, face your altar and say, "Blessed Be! Blessed Be the Gods! Blessed Be those who are gathered here." Finally, tap or knock on the altar with your knuckles (or wand) nine times in three series of three.

In the spring and summer, I suggest scattering flowers around the edge of your sacred circle to invite beauty and growth to your ritual, especially when doing love and sex magick.

The Four Directional Wards

After you have cast the circle, it is time to call the four directional Wards to stand guard and protect each of the thresholds of the four corners of your circle. The Wards, also called Watchtowers, are ancient and powerful beings of light who guard the elemental corners and keep negative energies from entering your ritual area.

Call the Wards in by starting at the North point. You can simply use your body, mind, and spirit when doing magick, or you can add focals such as magickal tools. When using your magickal tools, hold your athame in your right hand and a bowl of earth or salt in your left hand. Sprinkle three pinches of earth or salt at the North corner. When you are working with a partner, the male holds the tools and does the chants while the woman stands in the center of the circle and passes the elemental tools, i.e., athame, bowl, incense, candle, and chalice, back and forth from the altar to him.

After you have sprinkled the earth into the North corner, hold your athame high in your right hand and the bowl high in your left hand. Merge with the powers of the earth, arms raised high, and say, "Oh, great and mighty one, ruler of the North March, come, I pray you. Protect the gate of the North Ward. Come, I summon you!"

Moving to the East point, hold the incense in your hands and wave it back and forth three times in the East corner. Then hold the incense high in your left hand and your athame high in your right and say, "Oh, great and mighty one, ruler of the East March, come, I pray you. Protect the gate of the East Ward. Come, I summon you!"

At the South point, wave the candle three times in the South corner. Hold the candle high in your left hand and your athame high in your hand and say, "Oh great and mighty one, ruler of the South March, come, I pray you. Protect the gate of the South Ward. Come, I summon you!"

Moving to the West point, take the chalice of water and drip three drops of water into the West corner. Hold the chalice high in your left hand and your athame high in your right, saying, "Oh great and mighty one, ruler of the West March, come, I pray you. Protect the gate of the West Ward. Come, I summon you!"

Once the four directional Wards are called into the circle, cut a "Little Gate," which is an energetic entryway into the sacred circle. Do this with a sweep of your hand, just below the East point. Enter your circle through this gate and then close it again with a sweep of your hand once you are inside the circle.

Stand at the center of your sacred circle and begin chanting the names of the Goddess and God, "Kerridwen, Kerridwen, Kerridwen, Kernunnos, Kernunnos, Kernunnos, Ayea, Ayea, Ayea!" Build the intensity of the energy by swaying and circle dancing. Speak the names louder and louder, and then release the power as if you were shooting an arrow, directing it toward your magickal work. There are hundreds of Gods and Goddesses you can use to draw your sacred circle. I use Kerridwen and Kernunnos because I follow the Druid Path, but feel free to select appropriate Father Gods and Mother Goddesses, such as Odin and Freya, Isis and Osiris, from other pantheons.

Ward Markers, such as four clear quartz points, placed in the four directional corners or in other configurations around your sacred circle are practical and powerful ritual tools. Ward Markers are traditionally made of stone, wood, or metal. Painted or marked with symbols of the four directions, or inlaid with crystals and gemstones such as quartz, citrine, garnet, turquoise, amethyst, or moonstone, Ward Markers are then rubbed in scented oils and consecrated. Through time, and by being used again and again in ritual and ceremony, the energy of your Markers increases and can be used to solidify and amplify the energy in your sacred circle.

You can also use power animals as Guardians of your circle. Images, pictures, paintings, figurines, or other items related to power animals of the four corners are potent visual focals in magick. For example, you might place a picture of a whale or dolphin, or set up an aquarium in the West area of your sacred space, bluejay or peacock feathers in the East, a staff carved with a wolf's head in the North, and perhaps a figurine of a lion in the South. Use your imagination, selecting the power animals you have the strongest affinity with.

Heightening Love and Sex Magick With Focals

The components of magick include all of the things you use to achieve successful results. These include your altar, craft tools, all focals, and the actual work to be performed. Focals are chosen to coincide with your intention and are used both in the preparation of magick and for directing energy.

Use your intuition, blended with a little common sense, to check whether your focals coincide with your intention. For example, if you are doing healing work, I suggest you burn sage, cedar, and lavender incense to clear out negative energies and stabilize the healing area, rather than citrus or ylang-ylang, which may intensify the already imbalanced energies. Another example of matching your focals to your magickal work is paying attention to the color of the focals, for instance, candles. Use a white candle if you are working with the Goddess, a green candle for healing or prosperity, a pink or red candle for love, and so forth. As you continue practicing magick, you generally become better at gathering the best focals for your work.

When doing magick, fully engage your senses by using several focals, including, but not limited to, herbs, scented oils, candles, music, symbols, flowers, feathers, seashells, crystals, and gemstones, as well as incense, foods, chanting, textures, clothing, jewelry, and pictures.

Visual focals such as photographs, symbols, paintings, and tarot cards can be placed on the altar to help you to visualize and see your goals. Large clear quartz crystals or crystal spheres and pyramids, used for divination, are examples of common visual focals. Sex magick symbols, explained in Chapter 6, are uniquely useful visual focals, and I highly recommend using personally selected and/or created symbols for not only sex magick but in all of your magickal works.

Auditory focals, such as invocations, chants, songs, and music, help you reach deeper meditative and spiritual states of consciousness. The Egyptians called their hieroglyphs "the speech of the gods," while the Greeks revered the written word. The Druids felt that by knowing how to "spell" a word and speak it you had power over it. Anyone with the skill to capture sacred words and ritual on paper and who can speak these words is also capable of using this skill for successful magickal results. In ritual, oral and written focals in ritual serve to strengthen your magick. Remember to always say any chants, songs, spellwork, and pathworking aloud. The spoken word, like the written word, amplifies magickal energy and directs additional power and energy to your magickal patterns.

Playing a special song or musical piece while doing magick is advantageous for centering and focus. Your body, mind, and spirit learn to recognize a specific musical pattern and immediately associate it with magickal energy, prompting a quicker shift in awareness. Musicians often find themselves creating compositions that are magickal and have a mysterious effect on listeners. In tandem with music comes dancing and sacred movement, both of which widen your focus and deepen your meditative or magickal state of consciousness. The energy you build while dancing can be released and applied to your magickal patterns.

Your sense of smell is the sense tied closest to memory and has a direct effect on your instincts, feelings, and emotions. Every odor you perceive, whether pleasant or not, triggers minute chemical reactions in your brain that cause a reaction. Each smell carries messages, some conscious and some much deeper. Because of this, using scented oils gives you a stronger sensual focus that is particularly useful in love and sex magick. Fragrances from incense, fresh flowers, and scented oils all heighten your sensual and spiritual awareness. Using a certain fragrance when you do all of your magickal works is just like playing a particular piece of music each time you do magick. The fragrance, like the music, automatically and immediately triggers a magickal response and sets the tone for the work. (Refer to the Source Directory for vendors of useful focals.)

Tasting internalizes magick, because foods have a very real effect on you. For example, raspberries and strawberries are considered foods of love. With their natural sugars and sweetness, these fruits have an uplifting and energizing effect. Other sweet love foods like honey and whipped cream are famous in sex magick.

Touch increases your physical understanding of your intentions and desires. Soft, hard, coarse, smooth, warm, and cold are all registered by your body and mind. Because of this, sensation and touch can be used to enhance or activate your magickal patterns. For example, you may have a soft velvet magickal robe or tunic you wear when doing ritual. Merely touching the fabric may invoke a magickal state of awareness.

Love and Sex Magick Focals

VISUAL   Place a photograph, drawing, cards, letters, and other personal items of yourself and your beloved on or by your altar in a harmonious pattern. Lingham and yoni stones can be placed on your altar as symbols of sexuality and love. Paintings and sculptures depicting lovers embracing are also excellent visual love focals.

OLFACTORY   Anoint your altar tools, chair cushions, lightbulbs, and pillows with your special scent, and whenever in the company of your beloved always use this same fragrance or scent. You can also add a few drops of your signature fragrance to incense, along with love herbs, such as rosebuds and dried lavender flowers.

AUDITORY   Use soft romantic music and favorite songs when doing love and sex magick. Most New Age music is geared toward the spiritual and sensual, lending itself well to magick. If you play a musical instrument or sing you can use a specific melody or song when spinning your love and sex spells. The Celtic bards used music for magickal purposes in just such a way. Eastern mystical traditions use chanting as an auditory cue, which moves the followers to a higher or divine level of awareness. Humming and breathing can also be used to pattern magick, as can the natural sounds of bird songs, waterfalls, rain, and wind.

KINESTHETIC   What you wear and the colors, textures, and shapes of things surrounding you influence how you feel about yourself. Robes, special jewelry, masks, or going skyclad (nude) are ways to create a sacred feel to your magickal experience. For love and sex magick, if you are not going to work skyclad, I suggest you wear soft, fuzzy materials such as velvet, silk, soft cotton, or polar fleece in specifically selected colors. Also pay attention to the textures of items in your bedroom, such as pillows, satin sheets, down comforters, flowers, feathers, and so forth.

GUSTATORY   For thousands of years, people have been using powders, ointments, and charms to increase their sexual potency and desire. Aphrodisiacs increase desire, stamina, and intensity of experience, and increase the overall enjoyment of the sexual experience. Foods and beverages that vibrate with the energy of love and sex are apples, cherries, strawberries, peaches, apricots, grapes, pears, chocolate, ginger, nuts, parsley, lettuce, olives, avocados, tomatoes, honey, and whipped cream. Love and sex beverages include hibiscus, licorice, and nettle teas, wines, liqueurs, hot chocolate, fruit juices, and sparkling and hot cider. If you are going to use whipped cream, my suggestion is to whip up your own real cream to avoid the chemical additives in canned and container whipped cream.

Plant Magick

All natural objects have metaphysical uses and characteristics. Nature communicates her mysteries, as well as subtle energies, directly to us through color, smell, taste, sound, shape, and texture. Herbs are one of these mysteries—simple treasures for our use. The Hindus called herbs *yantras,* or sacred objects, and the ancients discovered that the basic hot and cold relationship of plants and diseases served as the fundamental principle of natural healing.

Likewise, Native Americans, considered herbs sacred gifts and would watch animals to learn which plants to eat for food and medicine. People of all cultures found that aromatic plants could be used for magick, medicine, and seasoning, and this herbal lore once formed the nucleus for scientific medicine. Remember, when you cook, be aware of the herbs you use and their flavorful and magickal qualities. For example, you may want to bake an apple-pecan cake for love, longevity, and abundance. (Apples serve as love charms and embody the tree of life and perpetual youth, or longevity. The pecan, like most nuts, represents fruitfulness and abundance.)

Herbs are beneficial to your entire being—body, mind, and spirit. Certain herbs contain life-enhancing qualities that relieve stress and tension. As you relax and your mind calms, your creativity increases, your body becomes energized, your mind feels clearer, and your spirit more connected to divine Oneness. Using herbs to raise the energy levels in your being by toning, cleansing, and nourishing enhances and strengthens your mental capabilities, and establishes a conscious connection with your higher self, just as using herbs in magick strengthens your magickal pattern.

Like herbs, flowers also have metaphysical uses and qualities. In Victorian times, flowers were used as a romantic language to express feelings and intentions between lovers. Today, a flower can be placed in a bud vase and kept by your telephone to remind you of your beloved and enhance your love and sex magick. Sending or bringing your loved one flowers reflects this tradition. The rose symbolizes love, while the periwinkle and chamomile represent friendship. The sunflower is for inspiration and used for sun magick, whereas the moonflower is for introspection and moon magick. Dandelions grant us wishes, and clover conveys good luck.

Colors of the flowers correspond to emotions. Red is the color of lust, sex, and virility; pink is friendship and companionship; white is sacred, pure, and spiritual love; blue is new beginnings and blue skies; green is love-growing and fertility; orange is the positive energy and power of love; purple is royal and noble love; and gold or yellow is shining, creative, and warm love.

In magick, releasing herbs or flowers to the wind or water, or burning herbs in incense, helps send energy toward your goal. Take care that your herbs and flowers are not harmful to the environment, pets, or other animals. Please refer to Appendix C: Love, Sex, and Magick Herbs, Flowers, and Resins for complete instructions for preparing herbal formulas, as well as the properties and uses of herbs, flowers, and resins used in magick.

Love and Sex Candle Magick

Candle magick provides a valuable and potent magickal process that is easy to perform. On a metaphysical level, candles are tools whose magickal qualities extend to the energetic, because the flame touches something deep within your being that connects to something within your spirit. The flame of the candle represents the spirit's highest potential, while the smoke carries your wishes, prayers, and desires to the divine.

Humans have known how to use fire for over five hundred thousand years. One legend says that Prometheus, son of the Titans, stole fire from the Gods and gave it to humankind. From that point on, people started lighting candles and using them to look into the future and influence patterns. From the flicker of divine light we gain a brief glimpse into the mysteries of the universe.

Practiced customarily on the Eight Great Days (Sabbats), full moons, and other holidays, candle magick is a powerful change element. For example, at Yule (Winter Solstice) a Yule fire, white candles, and electric lights are lit at the end of the ritual to symbolize the rebirth of the sun.

Candle magick is helpful in obtaining love, money, protection, well-being, good health, and good luck. Some say that melting wax into a burning candle melts the heart of your lover. Candle wax is also sprinkled throughout rooms for protection, pieces are placed inconspicuously inside special gifts and used to seal letters, magickal chants, and healing works.

Candle magick can be as simple as dedicating a candle to a special God or Goddess. For example, Kama, a beautiful young God whose name means desire, is the Hindu God of love and the first-born of the Mind. A powerful ally in love and sex, Kama carries a flower bow with a flower string and five magickal flower shafts. He holds mastery over everyone, and even the Gods are disordered when the spell of love touches them. This insures the perpetual creation of the world. Dedicating a candle to Kama brings you these qualities of love.

Making a simple dedication by lighting a candle in memory of an ancestor, or for a friend who has died, is a form of candle magick. Birthday candles are still used for making magickal wishes, and dreams and fantasies still come true during romantic candlelight dinners.

Candles come in all colors, shapes, and sizes. Match the color of your candle with your magickal goal. Please refer to Appendix A: Love and Sex Candle Magick for color correspondences. I work primarily with votives and tapers because they are reasonably priced and easy to obtain. Beeswax tapers that I roll myself from flat sheets, available from a local bee supply house, are my favorites. Not only do they smell honey-sweet when they burn, they are natural and are biodegradable. If you want to get fancy, there are specialty candles, such as phallus or Goddess candles, available from New Age and metaphysical shops that can be used for specific and obvious applications. Candles that are already scented, especially for love and sex magick, are also now available at New Age stores and can save you time in a pinch. (See the Source Directory for more information.)

If you are feeling creative, try making your own candles. Use beeswax, paraffin, natural dyes, or crayons. You can use old milk cartons, toilet paper rolls, or sand for molds, or buy premade candle molds from an arts and crafts supply store. (Make a sand candle mold by placing sand in a deep bowl or container or outside in a small pit. Simply hollow out the shape for the wax in the sand then pour the wax into the hollowed-out portion and position the wick. Once the wax hardens, remove the candle and brush off the sand.) Handcrafting your own candles for candle magick is particularly powerful. During each step of the process, merge with the ingredients and action of the procedure, placing your magickal intention, expectation, and desire into the candle itself. (To help you merge with the candle ingredients, take each ingredient, one at a time, and reflect upon it, asking yourself which element it represents. For example, the wax embodies the earth element and can be reshaped by fire. Take your time and notice what is unique about each ingredient, how it contributes to the whole, and so forth.)

Before beginning your candle-magick ritual, I suggest you take a ritual bath, using bath and sea salt. Spend as much time bathing as you want, using candlelight for illumination. Sprinkle a few drops of your favorite oil into your bath. After your bath, dress in your ritual robe or tunic and gather together everything you will need. Place the items on your altar table or other surface.

Begin dressing your candle by washing it in cool salt water and rinsing it. Carve names, initials, and symbols such as runes three times on the candle body using your athame, quill, or pen. Next, apply magickal oil to the candle body, covering it completely. Place the candle on your altar or other surface. (Refer to the listing of oils at the back of the book and select the appropriate one for your magickal work or ritual. The Source Directory supplies you with a list of retailers that sell oils. You can also purchase quality oils at most health food stores and local metaphysical and New Age shops. I use oils that I purchase and also those that I make myself. Last year I made a bottle of stargazer lily oil that was excellent for consecrating ritual and altar tools.)

Next, surround the candle in a circle of crystals and gemstones such as clear quartz, rose quartz, garnet, or citrine. Try several different patterns of stones, such as a pentacle, triangle, medicine wheel, and triple circle, and keep the directional corners in mind. Try using twelve stones that represent the twelve zodiac signs and then place them in a circle around your candle, or use stones to symbolize the planets and place these around your candle. Following is a list of astrological signs and corresponding gemstones:

Astrological Sign	*Gemstones*
Aries	Ruby, bloodstone, garnet, red jasper
Taurus	Carnelian, agate, lapis lazuli
Gemini	Aquamarine, clear quartz, agate, alexandrite
Cancer	Moonstone, milky quartz
Leo	Ruby, cat's-eye, carnelian, onyx, citrine, heliodor
Virgo	Sapphire, pink jasper, rose quartz, peridot
Libra	Opal, tourmaline, malachite
Scorpio	Garnet, ruby, agate, topaz, bloodstone
Sagittarius	Amethyst, blue topaz, hematite, turquoise, lapis lazuli
Capricorn	Beryl, onyx, garnet, obsidian
Aquarius	Sapphire, amethyst, aquamarine
Pisces	Bloodstone, jasper, jade, adventurine

All of these stones, when properly applied, embody the energies they represent and act as catalysts in magickal ritual.

Candle-magick stone grids are made of crystals and gemstones, positioned in specific patterns around the candle. For example, you can place a circle of tumbled rose quartz around a pink candle for love magick, or position a variety of stones around the candle in the form of a medicine wheel for healing, or in the shape of a pentagram for magickal powers. Use your imagination as to the shape and size of the grid.

Every time you form a grid you create an energy mandala. Because of this, a simple rule of thumb is to place the grid stones in harmonious and balanced positions according to size, shape, color, and so forth. Rely on your intuition, sensitivity, spiritual guidance, and experience when selecting and positioning grid stones.

Each grid contains a focal stone. Begin at the focal stone and visualize or sense connecting the grid stones together with an energetic silver or gold thread in a clockwise circle. Do this three times to strengthen the grid energy. When you are finished using the grid, upon the completion of your spellwork or ritual, pull up the grid stones in the reverse order in which you laid them down. Clean your stones before putting them away.

Carefully add selected herbs to your candle magick, sprinkling them inside the stone circle and on the candle itself. You can also add herbs to the candle flame. Please refer to Appendix C at the back of the book to select the most appropriate and effective herbs for your specific magickal work. For example, rose petals are perfect for love magick and handfasting rituals. Sage is excellent for healing, and bay can bring you prophetic dreams. Place other appropriate items from nature around your candle or inside your stone circle, such as flowers, shells, twigs, leaves, and rocks, as you desire.

Burning objects such as hair and nail clippings in the candle flame is the most familiar example of Contagious Magick, which is the magickal sympathy that is supposed to exist between a person and any severed portion of themselves, such as hair and nails. One of the first spells I did was a love spell by burning a strand of my lover's hair in a candle flame while meditating upon him.

Candles are excellent meditative aids, and burning candles works along the same pattern as all other magick, i.e., intention, expectation, desire, and merging. Using a metaphor to remember your spell as you merge with the flame is helpful, for example, "Here comes the bride" if you are doing a handfasting candle-magick spell for you and your beloved. Be sure to keep the intentions of your spell constantly in mind as you observe the flame of the candle. Making love by candlelight is still a popular tradition and helps to ensure the effectiveness of your love and sex candle-magick spells.

Candles speak a mystical language, with the words expressed by the flickering and dancing flame, the billowing of the smoke, and the popping and crackling of the hot wax. Candle chatter and the direction of the flame denote magickal communication. Each candle is unique and when lit reflects its own personality, communicated by the fire element, sometimes seen in mystical traditions as a small salamander encased within the flame.

Different parts of the candle and candleholder represent certain aspects of being. The flame of the candle symbolizes the soul or spirit. When lit, the wick is the vehicle of transmutation. The halo of the flame symbolizes divinity and God or Goddess/hood, while the body of the candle represents the physical properties, and when lit, embodies all of the elements. Please refer to Appendix A: Love and Sex Candle Magick for more love and sex candle-magick instructions and suggestions.

Love Spells and Charms

Love and sex charms and spells are based on homeopathic or imitative magick, working with images and the focals previously described. Magickal images have often been employed for the amiable purpose of winning love. For example, an ancient Hindu custom for securing one's affection was to shoot an arrow into the heart of a clay image of the person. Poppets were made to represent a husband and wife and then firmly tied together to symbolize and ensure the amity of the couple.

Charms and spellworking are essential parts of folk magick. To cast spells, use certain materials and tools in ritual to achieve specific results. Effective spellcasting is much the same as other magickal patterning, and the Three Eyes of Kerridwen (intention and expectation, desire, and merging) apply.

First, you need to be clear as to your intention and expectation. Always heed the Wiccan Rede of "Do what thou wilt, an' harm none," and use the elements of nature in beneficial and positive ways, for negative spellworking will only come back at you. The purpose and goal of your spell need to be clearly stated, preferably mentally, in writing, and with images such as photos, pictures, or drawings. Choose sponsor Goddesses, Gods, focals, and tools wisely, relying on your intuition and creativity when doing spell-work. Keep in mind that the greater the desire and need for the successful outcome of your spellworking, the better the chance for positive results. Cast out the necessary energy to bring about the needed result by merging with the successful outcome of your spellwork. Use deep breathing and visualization to direct the spell's energy out into the universe so it may become manifest. Become one with the divine, attuning with the Goddess and God and asking for guidance and insight. See, feel, hear, taste, touch, and intuit the successful outcome of the spellcasting.

Nine-Point Spell Checklist

1. Write down the kind of spell you are doing and for what purpose into a journal or Book of Shadows (a journal of magick spells, rituals, and other notes). Write down your expectation for the spellwork.
2. Note the date and time you cast the spell.
3. Note the significant corresponding astrological facts, such as the sun sign, moon phase, and so forth.
4. Select sponsor Goddesses and Gods, ancestors, power animals, guides, or other allies to help you in your spellwork.
5. Select a location to do your work. Consider casting love spells in your bedroom, in the woods, at the ocean, a river, nearby creek, or by a waterfall.
6. Make a list of all of the materials and any tools you will need for your spellwork and gather them together.
7. Cast the spell. Be sure to have easy-to-read instructions close by for reference while you are working.

8. Write down the results or your spellcasting. Remember, with some spells it may be necessary to wait a while to enter this information into your journal.

9. Write down any additional comments, suggestions, and other notes.

Following is a sampling of love spells and charms that everyone can have fun doing. Please refer to Appendix E: Love Spells and Charms for more magickal ideas and suggestions.

FEATHER CHARMS   Write a letter or send a card to your prospective mate with a white feather inside denoting your love and affection for him or her. Decorate the feather, perhaps by hand-painting the edges, or with glitter, ribbon, or colored string. Every action and attention you place on the feather will strengthen the effect of the charm. Be sure to receive feedback from your mate, for talking about the feather will reinforce the charm again. Use your personal scent on the feather to add another dimension to it. Be creative and use your imagination.

HAIR LOVE CHARM   Use a piece of your hair in a gift you make to give to your prospective mate. Sew it into a piece of clothing. Knit it into a scarf or sweater. Place a piece of your hair in a small locket and seal the locket shut, giving it to your mate as a necklace or key ring. The charm is even stronger if you can obtain a strand of your prospective mate's hair to put with yours in the locket. Place a piece of your hair in a card that you send. Leave a strand of your hair in your mate's car or house where it won't be disturbed. Keep the hair of your beloved in a locket around your neck, or a small pouch in your pocket.

LOVER'S CIRCLE   This is a love spell that consists of three circles of thread or cord and a total of thirty-nine colored beads. Cut three nine-inch lengths of thread, cord, or ribbon. Thread and knot thirteen colored beads (preferably red, rose, pink, peach, or lavender) on each string. Do not fasten the ends together yet.

Thread the ends of the three lengths through one large bead (red or gold), and tie the ends together in a firm knot to form a circle. All the while you are making your lover's circle, visualize your lover's face, body, and voice, tieing everything you like about your mate or prospective mate into your creation. Each bead represents one more aspect or quality about your lover that fascinates, intrigues, and pleases you. Carry your lover's circle with you, or place it in a conspicuous spot such as on the rearview mirror of your car, next to your working space, in the marriage corner or your bedroom Ba-Gua, or next to your bed. The more time you spend working with your lover's circle and concentrating on creating a positive relationship, the stronger the love magick.

6

Sacred and Divine Love, Sex, and Magick

I am One
We are Two
and then Three
Into infinity.
I am Six
You are Nine
Mirrored images
of the same Mind.
—Michael Starwyn

Everyone has the innate ability to connect with their female and male aspects, bringing themselves into balance and touching upon what the Goddess tradition calls "perfect love and perfect peace." The Goddess tradition, like tantra, realizes that when you truly make love you become the God and Goddess, connecting with the sacred and merging with divine light. You recreate infinity and become the boundless.

The ancients believed that without the actual sexual union between humans, trees, plants, and animals could not be fertile. Among certain African peoples, making love is ordained not only at calendar times relating to vegetation and harvest, but also as a means of reinvigorating the community at any time of distress, crisis, or need.

The sacred marriage was a serious magickal rite designed to make the woods grow green, the flowers bloom, and the grass sprout, as well as make the people, herds, and wildlife healthy and the fruits and vegetables grow. Handfasting, or sacred marriage, is still popular, and many couples find that once handfasted the sexual, mental, and spiritual elements of making love suddenly heighten and the experience becomes more intense because the bond takes on a divine quality. After you and your lover are handfasted, the physical, mental, and spiritual energy created when making love is probably the most powerful source of energy that human beings can generate, and this energy can be directed and used in meaningful ways.

My husband Michael and I chose Lughnassad, the Great Day during harvest time, for our handfasting. The reason for selecting this date was that we both have an affinity for the Celtic solar God, Lugh. Lughnassad literally means Lugh's wedding, and in the Gwyddonic Druid tradition it is the annual ritual when the nature Goddess Rosemerta weds the sun God Lugh. It is a time of fruition, harvest, and plenty, celebration, and joyful thanks.

Once we were handfasted, the nature of our relationship transformed in that our bond seemed stronger than ever and the feeling of sacred connection between us was more pronounced. For me, our handfasting ceremony was just as important as our legal marriage. I know many couples who are handfasted without being married, or are handfasted many months or years before they are legally wed because they place more importance on handfasting and sacred marriage.

Handfasting—The Sacred Rite of Union

The best days for handfasting rituals are the Eight Great Days of the Wheel of the Year when the seasonal cycles are at their peak. Handfastings are performed on the eve of the Great Day rather than on the day itself. Beltane, or May Day, is always a favorite time for handfastings because spring is in the air and nature is at her most sensuous and sexual.

You can also choose to be handfasted on one of the full moons. Before selecting a moon, examine the nature and qualities of all the thirteen moons and then pick the one that most represents your bond with your lover. An ideal day for the Ritual of Union is when a Great Day and High moon overlap. This happens generally once or twice a year and has the effect of doubling the universal energy, both solar and lunar, for your handfasting ceremony and lovemaking. I suggest you use an ephemeris (the pocket versions are handy), which makes it a lot easier to precisely calculate the Great Days and High moons. Also, please refer to the listing of the Great Days and full moons in the previous chapter.

Prior to the handfasting ceremony, you and your mate need to gather together all of the items that go into your marriage box. The box can be simple or elaborate, and is customarily kept in a conspicuous place in your bedroom after your handfasting. I keep our small carved sandstone marriage box on our bedroom dresser. Traditional marriage box items include the following:

The woman brings a small white feather, a bag of seven different spices, and a small bag of seeds.

The man brings a smooth white pebble, a small bundle of seven different woods, and three silver coins.

Also needed are two pieces of yarn—a nine-inch piece of red yarn and an eight-inch piece of green yarn—as well as a small bottle of scented oil, such as patchouli, lavender, amber, or rose.

For me, collecting the items for our marriage box was an intriguing part of the adventure. We examined coins from coin shops and collected silver dollars from Nevada while on a trip across the United States. We found seeds, spices, and pieces of wood from twenty-one different states, a smooth white pebble by a secluded lake in Hope, New York, and a white feather by the Mississippi River. (Please refer to the Source Directory for suppliers of decorative boxes.)

Handfasting Ritual of Union

The Ritual of Union is performed with great care, for the woman and man do become the Goddess and God for a short time. You may think this impossible, but I assure you that is exactly what happens. In the Druid tradition there is a saying, "To know oneself is to know deity, and to know deity is to know oneself."

Please note that if you are performing a same-sex handfasting ritual, merely insert the word *mate* or *spiritual partner* for the words *wife* and *husband*. Also insert *man* or *woman*, depending upon the situation. If you both intend on being aspects of the Goddess who are joining as one, repeat the "Sacred Nature" passage for the Goddess, and vice versa if you both intend on being aspects of the God.

Likewise, if you are performing a handfasting ritual with more than two persons, be sure to adapt the ritual accordingly, repeating the woman and man parts as needed to include all of those being handfasted. For example, if two men and two women are being handfasted, then repeat the questions so that everyone has a chance to say their vows to each other. I advise mapping this out beforehand to avoid any confusion or delays in the ceremony itself.

The Ritual of Union is customarily performed by a High Priestess and High Priest, but since these officials are not always available or known, I have adapted the ritual that follows so couples can handfast themselves. This is the exact handfasting ritual that my husband and I did together, and is adapted from the Great Book of the Gwyddonic Druid Tradition. Remember that your souls are twinned in the sacred marriage of love, and feel free to modify and add to the ritual.

Before the handfasting ritual begins, set up the altar. Place the items that represent the Goddess on the left, or feminine side, and the items symbolizing the God on the right, or masculine side. Place your marriage box in the center of the altar, together with the two pieces of yarn and the other marriage box items. Handfasting rings, like the knot, act as a spiritual bond. If you choose to exchange rings, place them on the altar next to your marriage box. Any additional words that you may want to say to each other need to be written down and placed where you can read or reach them easily. If you plan on playing a song on a guitar, harp, or other musical instrument, make sure the instrument and music is close to your altar.

Once you are ready to begin, light the altar candles and the incense. Using the instructions in Chapter 5, draw the sacred circle and call in the four directional Wards. After you call in the Wards, cut an energetic Little Gate just below the East point of your circle. With your lover, step through this energetic gate into the center of the circle. The instructions follow:

Handfasting Ceremony

(Adapted from the Great Book of the Gwyddonic Druid Tradition)

The man asks the woman: Are you one who respects and honors the Earth, Sun, and Stars, and do you love the God and Goddess?

The woman answers: Yes! Praise be!

The woman asks the man: Are you one who respects and honors the Earth, Sun, and Stars, and do you love the God and Goddess?

The man answers: Yes! Praise be!

The man asks: Why have you come here, and what do you seek?

The woman answers: I have come here to seek union with you, and the blessing of the Goddesses and Gods upon our union.

The woman asks: Why have you come here, and what do you seek?

The man answers: I have come here to seek union with you, and the blessing of the Goddesses and Gods upon our union.

The man says to the woman: My love, it is said of the Goddess: "Thou art every wife and every wife art thou! Thou art every lover and every lover art thou!" Do you seek this union with the full knowledge of its sacred nature?

The woman answers: Yes! Blessed Be!

The woman asks: My Love, it is said of the God: "Thou art every husband and every husband art thou. Thou art every lover and every lover art thou!" Do you seek this union with the full knowledge of its sacred nature?

The man answers: Yes! Blessed be!

The woman brings the marriage box from the altar.

The man asks: Show me what you have brought as a pledge of your intent.

The woman shows the man the small white feather, a bag of seven different spices, and a small bag of seeds and puts them in the box.

The woman asks: Show me what you have brought as a pledge of your intent.

The man shows the woman the smooth white pebble, a small bundle of seven different woods, and three silver coins before putting them in the box. The woman sets the open marriage box back on the altar.

The woman asks: Show me your true intent with the yarn of union.

With his red yarn, the man ties a knot around the green yarn of the woman, and she ties a knot around his red yarn. The man carefully places the yarn of union in the marriage box, and the woman closes the lid and places it on the altar.

The woman and man face each other, hold hands, and say together: Before the God and Goddess and all who are gathered here, we have shown our true intent.

The woman takes the scented oil from the altar and traces a five-pointed star encircled by a heart on the man's forehead. Then the man takes the oil and traces a five-pointed star encircled by a heart on the woman's forehead.

The woman and man face each other, hold hands once again, and say together: In the name of the Gods, Blessed Be this union! In Oneness, Blessed Be our union! Praise be and thanks to the Goddess and God! Blessed Be!

Toasting the Gods and Feasting

After the Handfasting Ritual of Union it is customary to toast the Goddesses and Gods. Fill your glasses or teacups and select your favorite Goddesses and Gods to honor. Feasting is also traditional, so be sure to prepare some of your favorite foods, especially some of the love foods I have suggested. Take plenty of time to enjoy your feast, feeding each other finger foods such as grapes, berries, nuts, and candies. During this time, tell your lover how much you care about him or her. Through words and actions, show how deep your love goes. Discuss what it means to be the Goddess and God for a time, how it feels, and what your dreams for your future together are.

As you may have already guessed, consummating the Ritual of Union is the best part of the ceremony. If you are working with a group, you will probably want to wait until you get home or your company departs. In that case, you will close the circle. When you are performing the handfasting ritual with your partner, or solo with a divine lover, in the privacy of your home or in a secluded spot in nature, physically making love is the natural next step. Leave the circle open because it will protect you during your lovemaking experience and at the same time amplify your every sensation. I also recommend that you read through this chapter and apply any or all of the sex magick techniques suggested.

When making love after your handfasting, see and sense yourself and your lover as Goddess and God. You may want to select the name of a Goddess or God for this experience and chant it as you climax. Doing so keys in on and embodies particular aspects of divinity. Use your intention and breath to reach the state just before orgasm, and then see and sense yourself and your lover being surrounded by a sphere of brilliant white light. You connect and climax in the light, as it expands outward in every direction, at which time you become one with each other and the universe. Even though your handfasting ritual is a very serious and sacred occasion, remember to have fun, keep a sense of romance and humor, and be creative.

At the end of the festivities, thank the Goddess and God and pull up the sacred circle by holding your right hand (or athame or wand) in front of you and visualizing the blue-white light of the circle being pulled into the palm of your hand as you slowly turn in a 360-degree counterclockwise circle. Knock three times on the altar to release the Wards. The Handfasting Ritual of Union is then complete.

Breaking the Union

If the two people who have entered into the Ritual of Union in good faith come to see that they are truly ill suited to each other, they can bring their marriage box out, take back their objects, and burn the yarn of union. By doing so they sever their spiritual bond and are free of one another.

Sacred Sex

Desire is central to the expansion of body, mind, and spirit, and needs to be given more attention in relationships accordingly. Within your sexual imagination, the spirit is alive and fertile, excited and adventuresome. Life-shaping events are frequently motivated by desires and attractions. Something eternal, invisible, yet very real comes to you in your perceptions, sensations, and the emotions of love, romance, and sex.

When life becomes erotic the spirit becomes involved in the experience. Sex brings magick into a relationship, deepening the connection between lovers in a way that talking or doing things together never can. Sexual love, or Eros, is often viewed in the context of being divine, sacred, and holy, in that it is the power that weaves us together and stimulates our inherent desire to merge with the Beloved, both the human and sacred Beloved.

Sacred sex is a lot hotter than physical sex. You move beyond physical sensation and fantasy and into the spiritual realm, where all things are possible. A divine sexual experience changes you permanently because it transforms you and your perceptions, including those of your relationship, yourself, and your lover.

Tantra adepts called *tantrikas* know that each of us is a being of light, with both a physical and an energetic body. Sacred sexual practices such as the Sacred Sex Wine Ceremony, which follows, and the sex-magick techniques, which follow later in this chapter, are ways to heighten your awareness of your energy body. This unlocks and opens up powerful energetic pathways within your body, supplying you with more light, empowering you and affecting every aspect of your life.

Sacred Sex Wine Ceremony

By symbolizing divine love and union of the Goddess and God, this ceremony reaffirms the merging and mating of female and male energies. You will need: 1. a chalice, cup, or glass; 2. an athame or sword (double-sided) or a wand; 3. wine or other beverage; and 4. at least one hour of privacy. In representing the sharing of the essence and spirit of the Goddess, the Sacred Sex Wine Ceremony literally and figuratively joins lovers together, bringing them closer. I use the names of Celtic deities, Kerridwen and

Kernunnos, but you can just as well use Egyptian, Greek, Roman, African, or Mesoamerican deities, such as Isis and Osiris, Hera and Zeus, Jupiter and Juno, Oshun and Shango, and Ometecutli and Omecihuatl. The important thing is to choose a prominent and powerful, preferably sensuous, Mother Goddess and Father God from whichever pantheon you prefer.

Wine is the customary liquid used in this ceremony, and obviously the alcohol content serves to relax the participants. If you drink only nonalcoholic beverages you can substitute grape juice, sparkling cider, or any other favorite beverage for the wine. When you drink wine from the same vessel you share the same essential light, and become one. So come together with your lover and drink the nectar of life, savoring every sweet droplet with succulent desire.

Direct eye contact is crucial in this ceremony. By really gazing into your lover's eyes you bring them inside of you, and they become part of you for a few moments. These moments of recognition into the soul of your lover can also bring you self-knowledge.

Set up the altar appropriately with the above-mentioned items. Include other items such as incense, wine-colored candles, flowers, and so forth. Be creative and wear wine-colored clothing or go skyclad and finger paint wine-colored designs on each other's bodies. Draw a sacred circle around the ceremonial space, including the altar and something comfortable to make love on (a bed, cushions, a futon, or sofa). Then enter in together through the Little Gate.

Traditionally, the man opens the wine and the woman fills the chalice, holding the vessel firmly between both of her hands. The man takes his athame, sword, or wand and sinks it slowly and deliberately, tip first, into the cup of wine, while saying:

> *Great and mighty ones,*
> *Let thy blessing and power*
> *Enter into this wine!*
> *So, mote it be!*

The woman hands the filled chalice to the man. Taking it, he carefully lifts the cup upward toward the North point (usually where your altar is set up), and says:

> *Ayea! Ayea! Kerridwen!*
> *Ayea! Ayea! Kernunnos!*
> *Ayea! Ayea! Ayea!*

He then turns clockwise to the East and does the same; likewise to the South and West. Upon completion of the circle, he returns to the North point and the altar, where he says:

> *Blessed Be!*
> *Blessed Be the Gods!*
> *Blessed Be all who are gathered here!*

Taking a sip of the wine, he then passes it to the woman while saying to her, "Perfect love and perfect peace." She drinks from the chalice, hands it back to her lover, and then says to him, "Perfect love and perfect peace." They exchange the chalice in this manner until there is only one remaining sip. The man takes the last sip, emptying the chalice, and sets the cup back on the altar. Together the lovers loudly say, "Blessed Be!"

The woman fills the chalice again and carries it over to the bed and sets it down. Staying within the sacred circle, the lovers embrace and begin kissing and sensually caressing each other. In a reclining position, the woman takes the cup of wine and sprinkles a few drops on her lover's erect phallus. The man then takes the cup of wine and sprinkles a few drops on the woman's breasts, stomach, and thighs. The man sets the wine down. The woman then places her hands on either side of her yoni, her sacred vessel. As the lovers look into one another's eyes, the man holds his lingham (wand of light) and guides it slowly between her hands and into her completely. Slowly he circles his wand inside of her clockwise, nine times, all the while looking directly into his lover's eyes. The woman and man make love slowly, continuing to gaze into each other's eyes. Just as the lovers begin to climax, and all during orgasm, they repeat the following words again and again together, adding their own names and special words of endearment:

Ayea! Ayea! Kerridwen!
Ayea! Ayea! Kernunnos!
Ayea! Ayea! Ayea!

After orgasm, the woman takes the chalice of wine and hands it to her lover. He takes a drink from the cup and passes it back to her. Then she takes a sip and hands it back to him. They do this until the cup has one sip remaining. The man finishes it and places the chalice back on the altar. Then together, the lovers loudly say, "Blessed Be!"

Moving Sexual Energy

As with your senses, your chakras also transmit energy, particularly when they are highly stimulated and activated. With practice, you can become skilled at directing this chakra energy outward at will.

Sex is one of the means for triggering your chakras, as well as generating large amounts of energy that can be outwardly directed. Merging is the point where the ideal, the real, and the divine meet. When you become one with your lover during intercourse, you establish a divine connection and surplus of useful energy that waits to be moved in a myriad of ways.

Sex is a fire that generates an insurmountable power whose extent knows no bounds. When you become intimate with your partner, moving your experience and bond into the spiritual, your relationship takes on divine qualities. When you and your partner run energy and light through each of your chakras while making love, you generate an immense amount of energy that, through intention, can be used to raise the harmonic of your body, mind, and spirit. By moving the powerful energy of lovemaking upward through your chakras, focusing your awareness on each chakra, one at a time, you can actually direct it for specific purposes, such as healing and the successful outcome of your patterns.

Raising your harmonic by running sexual energy through your chakras is a way of bringing more magick into your relationship. The sexual dimension permeates every aspect of your life, both on a conscious and subconscious level. In addition, sex gives rise to much of life's poetics, coming in the form of paintings, musical compositions, books, gardens, and other creations of the heart. These poetics extend into the intimacies of relationships. Like a great work of art, when your relationship becomes magickal, it reaches into and touches the creative source for inspiration.

Running the Light

Love is light and light is love. Loving and positive patterns generate loving and positive energy. If there were no love, there would be no light because love is what illuminates life. Love is the light in which we see each thing in its true origin, image, nature, and destiny. Unless you see someone or something in the light of love, you do not see them or it at all.

In the sacred sexual experience, sensation and awareness expand, propelling you into ecstasy and bliss. As you run the light, you completely let go and fly into Oneness.

Method 1: Running the Light for Women

1. Lie down comfortably and ground and center yourself.
2. Visualize and feel a bright, golden sun hovering about two feet above your head.
3. Breathe in and inhale the warm golden light of the sun through the top of your head, down your torso, through your arms, hands, legs, and feet.
4. Move the light slowly through the center of your body, brightening and clearing your energetic pathways.

5. Fill your body with golden sunlight, allowing the light to travel from the top of your head down to your pineal and pituitary glands, to your thyroid in your throat, to your thymus, behind both breasts and over your nipples, through your adrenals and kidneys and into your ovaries. Moving your hands slowly over these areas of your body helps to enhance the experience.

6. Allow the warm golden sunlight to spread throughout your body, and bask in your own female power and energy.

Method 2: Running the Light for Men

1. Lie down comfortably and ground and center yourself.

2. Visualize and feel a bright, golden sun hovering about two feet above your head.

3. Breathe in and inhale the warm golden light from the sun, through the top of your head, down your torso, through your arms, hands, legs, and feet.

4. Move the light slowly through the center of your body, brightening and clearing your energetic pathways.

5. Fill your body with golden sunlight, allowing the light to travel from the top of your head, down to your pineal and pituitary glands, to your thyroid and thymus, down through your adrenals and kidneys to your prostate. Moving your hands slowly over these areas of your body greatly enhances the experience.

6. Allow the warm golden sunlight to spread throughout your body, and bask in your own male power and energy.

Method 3: Running Musical Light (for Men and Women)

Put on your favorite piece of music. Focus your attention on your chest and stomach. Imagine a huge ball of powerful white light there, and, as you breathe, the ball becoming brighter and fuller. As you exhale, intentionally move the light up your chakras and out your crown chakra to your desired destination. This is one way to use your breath and mind together to direct the energy generated in lovemaking toward a particular outcome. When doing this with musical accompaniment, breathe to the rhythm of the music and sense yourself drinking in, circulating, and absorbing the energy of the music throughout your entire body. Use the rhythm of the music to help direct the sexual energy to its destination.

For me, using different kinds of music helps me clear the energetic pathways of my body, with the rhythm and tones of the music setting the pace for sex magick. For relaxing and breathing deeply into your body, choose something slow and melodic to begin with, moving on to more rhythmic and erotic musical selections as you progress through the sex magick process.

Sex Magick

Modern sex magick was introduced in Europe and the United States by two men, an American called Pascal Beverley Randolph and the English magician Aleister Crowley. Randolph studied the magickal traditions of the Middle East and Europe and created a method of sex magick drawn primarily from Tibetan sources, while Crowley gathered his information from an English magickal order that followed Rosicrucian, Masonic, and Kabbalistic sources. Now Eastern (tantric) and Western (Wiccan) sex magick practices are coming to the forefront once again.

Sex magick is based on the belief that the most powerful moment of human existence is the orgasm, or climax. Sex magick is the art of utilizing sexual orgasm and the energy from climax to enhance or create a reality while also expanding your consciousness. You can actively use the energy of sex to manifest your personal goals of desire. All senses and psychic powers are heightened during sexual climax. It is the moment when a door opens to the unlimited well of energy of the boundless. All you need to do is allow yourself to step through the threshold.

During sex magick, it is necessary to maintain your focus and then channel the energy into creating something—a more positive relationship, a better job, a more satisfying sex life, higher spiritual awareness, and so on. Your only limit is your imagination.

Intention and breath are the two key elements to successful sex magick. First, examine and focus your intention on exactly what you want to accomplish in your sex magick experience. Second, use your breath to relax your entire body from your head to your toes, and from your toes to your head. To do this, inhale while visualizing and sensing a cobalt blue light washing you from head to toe, moving from the top of your head down to your neck, shoulders, arms, hands, back, chest, stomach, through your lower back and pelvis, down your thighs, legs, ankles, and feet. Reverse the fluid light, moving it from the bottoms of your feet upward through your thighs, pelvis, stomach, back, shoulders, arms, and hands, and upward across your chest and the back of your neck, all the way up through your face and out the top of your head. After you have washed yourself out with this energetic blue light, use pink or red light, tuning your body energy to a more sexual harmonic.

The best time for sex magick depends on what you want to accomplish. Generally, if you are working toward a goal or creating something, the Eight Great Days and thirteen full moons are the strongest energy times to do sex magick. Other holidays such as anniversaries and birthdays are also excellent times for sex magick rituals. I advise against doing these rituals during dark moon phases unless you are trying to rid yourself of a negative relationship, bad habit, or other shadow affliction. My experience has been that waxing moon phases are better suited to sex magick than waning moon phases.

Create a magickal space in your bedroom, in a secluded, legal, and safe spot in nature, or in that special hideaway by the coast or in the mountains. Decorate your magickal space with white, pink, and red flowers, and dress your bed in satin or flannel sheets. Drape a velvet comforter over your bed or sacred area. Burn amber and lavender incense, and play soft sexy music. Candles always add a romantic light to any sexual encounter, and I suggest you experiment using the many scented candles available. Use your signature scented oil on your candles before you burn them, rubbing a thin film of oil over the wax body of the candle. For more specific kinds of candles to be used in sex magick, plus additional suggestions, please refer to Appendix A: Love and Sex Candle Magick.

Bathing or showering is encouraged, followed by a massage with scented oil. When doing sex magick with your lover, bathe or shower together and give each other a sensuous massage. You can make your own scented massage oil by adding a few drops of pure vanilla extract to a quarter cup of almond or olive oil. With scented oil, anoint your heart, both of your ankles, wrists, behind each of your ears, and the back of your head. Do the same for your lover.

As in all rituals, the preliminary steps in sex magick are setting up your altar, drawing the sacred circle, and calling in the four directional Wards. When setting up your altar for sex magick, you need two sex power objects, male and female. (Examples of male power objects are a crystal, stone, piece of wood, or other item in the form of a phallus. A woman's sex power object might be a seashell, crystal geode or egg, a flower, a piece of rounded wood, or a stone with an opening in the center.) The male object is placed on the right side of the altar and the female power object on the left, perhaps on either side of a vase of flowers or a potted plant.

Sex Magick Process

1. Identify what you want to enhance or create. When doing sex magick with your lover, be sure you agree beforehand what you want to direct your sexual energy toward. It is important that you choose something you truly desire. Be specific about what you are creating, and try to keep it simple.

2. Write out what you are creating in the style of a positive affirmation, phrasing it as if it were already so. For example, when working with your partner, say, "Our sex life is more loving, exciting, and sacred every day."

3. Compose a simple one-line chant, mantra, or song, incorporating your affirmation. Phrasing your composition in the present, use your voice to build even more power into the process. Place this on your altar.

4. Draw, paint, computer animate, or construct a symbol that represents your desired creation and the essential vision of your intended experience. For example, you might use two spirals coming together, two connected hearts, or a yoni and lingham combined with a symbol that represents what you intend to create during sex magick. Place this on your altar and next to your bed.

5. Focus on your affirmation and symbol. Feel, hear, taste, touch, see, and intuit it. Become it by merging with the successful desired outcome. As if you have stepped into the future, see and sense yourself already experiencing your desired creation. Walk through the door to the future and be there for a few minutes, with all of your concentration focused on the image of the future. Breathe your intention into this movie in your mind, using your breath to get more detailed images and sensations.

6. Do whatever it is that brings you almost to a climax. This can be any kind of sexual activity, with a supportive partner or solo.

7. Breathe into this preorgasmic state. Take your time. Reach this state of almost orgasm at least three times, with an optimum being nine times. With a little practice, it becomes easier to control your orgasm(s). The idea is not to climax yet.

8. Focus your mind on your creation, affirmation, and magickal symbol. In your mind, make it as vivid and real as possible. Imagine your magickal symbol becoming bigger and bigger, until the symbol seems to encircle you completely. When you finally do climax, keep focused on your symbol, seeing and sensing the picture, creation, or sensation that you want to experience in the future.

9. Now gaze into your lover's eyes (if you are with a partner) and deliberately move all of the energy of climax, the energy in your body, the energy surrounding your body, and the power of

your mind toward the desired outcome. Let it all flow into your creation and into the reality where you are actually experiencing the successful outcome. Use your breath to drive and move the energy into your creation, affirmation, and symbol. Stretch this out for as long as you can.

You will want to make several copies of your sex magick symbol and place them in conspicuous places in your home—on the refrigerator door, the bathroom mirror, and the back of your front and back doors—so the symbol is the last thing you see as you leave your home. Spend a few minutes each day focusing on your sex magick symbol, visualizing your intended creation growing bigger and bigger, filling the image with light and energy. If you find you want to cancel your creation, simply burn your symbol and bury or dispose of the ashes.

Sex Magick Guided Journey

The following creative sex magick journey exemplifies how sexual energy can be focused and directed:

She takes his naked body into hers, and they sense an explosion of energy emanating from their hips and pelvic area. Like a warm glow of sunlight, she feels his desire heat up as he thrusts himself deep within the impressions of her first chakra.

At first they concentrate on the energy building within her yoni as it meets his lingham, until both of them pulsate and vibrate with an energy that seems all-consuming. At the juncture when their movements become one, the lovers begin to move the energy up into their second chakras. She begins to tremble as he moves faster and faster inside of her. They use their deep rhythmic breathing to move the energy up into their solar plexus chakras and then into their heart chakras.

She speaks his name and moans her appreciation as he strokes her breasts. All the while, the lovers focus on moving the energy upward into their throat chakras. Communicating words of endearment, their bodies and energies entwine and she feels the light move up into her sixth chakra. It is as if her third eye opens and meets his simultaneously, becoming one. Flesh into flesh, spirit into spirit, they each flow into the other. Through the chakras, they continue to move and gather the energy upward into their crown chakras.

Suddenly everything intensifies a hundredfold. Together, they run the light up their chakras countless times, while their intercourse of energy continues to build higher and higher. Simultaneously they travel together in unison, running the energy and light from one chakra to another a final time, until they reach the top of their heads. They focus the power and force of their lovemaking and direct it outward, directing and releasing their powerful loving energy toward their desired goal and intended pattern. They feel the magick rush in like waves of the ocean, soaking and refreshing their souls.

Full Moon Sex Magick

When doing Full Moon Sex Magick with your lover, greet him or her with a glass of wine or other beverage, taking a sip and handing the glass over, and vice versa. When doing magick together the customary greeting is "Merry Meet and Merry Part; Perfect Love and Perfect Peace." This greeting sets the pace of the ritual and lovemaking to come.

The Full Moon Sex Magick Process, which follows this section, is geared for couples, a man and a woman. With a little creativity, you can adapt the process when working solo, with a same-sex lover, or with more than two people. In modern ritual, both women and men draw down the powerful lunar energy of the full moon to focus and direct it in Full Moon Sex Magick.

The purpose of drawing down the moon for sex magick is to gain knowledge and power directly from the Goddess, especially from those deities that are related to moon magick, such as Kerridwen (Celtic), Isis (Egyptian), Artemis (Greek), and Diana

(Roman). The manner in which it is presented here is also a form of pathworking because you ask a question of the Moon Goddess. Keep in mind that there are also male Gods related to the moon, which can be drawn down in this basic manner. No hard and fast rules apply, as male deities also embody and express the qualities of the moon.

Use plenty of focals in Moon Sex Magick, such as dreamy background music, love foods like marshmallows, special lighting, and moon-related symbols such as the crescent moon and star. Set up your altar in your own way, with the instructions within easy reach. Traditional altar tools usually include a chalice, wand, athame (sword), bowl, candleholder and candle, incense burner and incense, and objects that represent the Goddess, God, ancestors, and nature spirits. Keep in mind that the focals you choose to include in your ritual, the way you draw your circle, and how you perform the preliminaries all influence the ritual's final outcome.

Beforehand, create a symbol for your Moon Sex Magick ritual. When doing sex magick with your lover, create the symbol together. The symbol can be elaborate, full-color, and poster size, or be drawn with a pen or pencil on a piece of paper, or with a stick on the ground when making love outdoors. The symbol represents your Moon Sex Magick goal—what it is you are going to focus and direct your sexual energy toward. The Goddess or God you will be drawing down into your being needs to be represented somewhere in the body of the symbol.

The Moon Sex Magick ritual that follows requires a comfortable place for lovemaking—a private spot where you will not be disturbed. Unplug the phone or turn on your answering machine (volume off), and lock the door. If you are outdoors, make certain you have everything you will need for the ritual gathered in a bag or box, including ritual tools, instructions and a script, a quilt or large pad, matches, a bottle opener, music tapes and player, candles, incense, scented oil, foods, and so forth.

I suggest you engage in Moon Sex Magick after a light and tasty supper by candlelight. A moonlit picnic in a secluded garden is also a good choice. This supper is followed by a warm and sensuous bath scented with vanilla, lemon, sandalwood, or mint oil. Remember, in lovemaking you will be tasting a bit of the oil on the surface of your lover's skin, so I recommend the scented oil be organic and a flavor or scent both you and your lover can savor. After bathing, towel each other off slowly and sensuously, and then dress in moon colors and textures, such as ivory silk and lace, or soft white cotton. Allow yourself to enjoy the spirit of the ritual and have fun.

Moon Sex Magick Process

1. Set up your altar, preferably where moonlight spills on it, light the candles and incense, and turn on the music. As you light the candles and incense, dedicate them to the Moon Goddess with whom you will be working magick, and to the love between you and your lover. Place your Moon Sex Magick symbol in plain view. Draw the sacred circle and call in the four directional Wards, as explained in the previous chapter.

2. Position yourself so you are looking at the full moon out the window, or, if you are fortunate, in a safe location outdoors where you can see the moon easily and its beams can shine directly on you and the ritual area. Breathe in to the count of three and visualize inhaling the moonlight, hold your breath for three counts, and then exhale for three counts. Breathe this way, now and again, throughout the ritual to relax and center yourself.

3. Undress slowly and sensuously for each other. In this ritual you will work skyclad. Rub your hands together briskly to build a field of energy. Anoint your lover with lavender, lemon, or rose oil. Dab oil on the skin on the insides of both of your ankles, both wrists, the back of both ears, and on the back of your head where your skull meets your spine, heart, and third eye, always moving from the ground upward. Briefly rub and caress the anointed areas as you apply the oil.

4. In the center of the sacred circle, the man stands in front of

the woman, who has her arms outspread. The man and woman then call down the essence of the Moon Goddess into them. Begin chanting aloud in unison the name(s) of the Goddess (or God) whose power you are drawing down. For example, "Ayea, Ayea, Anu!" Keep chanting the name or names slowly and clearly, building up the energy and sensing the divine connection with the Goddess and the moon.

5. Still facing one another, the man gives the woman the Five-fold Blessing:

"Blessed Be your feet that have led you to me."
He then kneels down and slowly and sensuously kisses her right foot and then her left.

"Blessed Be your knees that kneel at the sacred altar."
He kisses her right knee softly and then her left knee.

"Blessed Be your womb without which we would not exist."
He kisses her sensuously and slowly just above her pubic hair.

"Blessed Be your breasts, symbols of perfect love and beauty."
He stands and kisses her right breast and then her left breast.

"Blessed Be your lips that speak the sacred words of love."
He kisses her fully on the mouth, and the lovers embrace.

6. Facing one another again, the woman gives the man the Fivefold Blessing:

"Blessed Be your feet that have led you to me"
She then kneels down and slowly and sensuously kisses his right foot and then his left.

"Blessed Be your knees that kneel before me and at the sacred altar."
She kisses his right knee softly and then his left knee.

"Blessed Be your manhood without which we would not exist."
She kisses him sensuously and slowly just above his phallus.

"Blessed Be your breasts, symbols of perfect peace and strength."
She stands and kisses his right nipple and then his left.

"Blessed Be your lips that speak the sacred words of love."
She kisses him fully on the mouth, and the lovers embrace at length.

7. Focus on your Moon Sex Magick symbol and concentrate on evoking the divine energy, spirit, and wisdom of the Moon Goddess. Actually visualize and feel the energy of the moon flowing into you as if you are drinking in the moonlight. Swallow the boundless, and imagine you and your lover becoming the moon, with moonlight radiating outward from your skin, head, pelvis, hands, and feet.

8. The man puts a dab of scented oil on his right forefinger and touches the woman on her left breast, right breast, womb, and left breast. He says, "I invoke the power of the Moon Goddess into this loving woman." He then puts a small amount of oil on the palms of both of his hands, rubs them together briskly, and then slowly strokes his lover's body downward with both hands from her breasts to her feet, kneeling as he reaches her feet. He kisses her left foot and then her right foot, and says, "I adore and love you, forever and a day."

9. The woman puts the scented oil on her left forefinger and touches the man on his right breast, left breast, phallus, and right breast. She says, "I invoke the power of the Moon Goddess into this loving man." She then puts a few drops of oil on the palms of both of her hands, rubs them together briskly, and then slowly strokes her lover's body downward with both hands from his shoulders to his feet, kneeling before him as she reaches his feet. She kisses his left foot and then his right foot, and says, "I adore and love you, forever and a day."

10. You embrace and make love, merging as deeply as you can with deity and peaking the energy within and outside of your body. Strengthen your focus by using deep rhythmic breathing. Just before you climax, focus on sending your sexual energy

toward the Moon Sex Magick symbol. Say together, "We are one, we are one, we are one," over and over again, and purposefully direct the sexual light and excitement. As you chant with your lover, allow the orgasmic energy to come through you and flow into its destination. When the energy has stopped flowing out-ward toward your sex magick goal, say in unison, "So be it."

11. Relax and lay back for a few minutes and allow any images, impressions, or sensations to flow through you as you qui-etly gaze and merge with the light of the moon. Silently ask one question of the Moon Goddess, one related to your Moon Sex Magick goal. After you receive an answer, thank the Goddess.

12. Toast the Goddesses and Gods, making sure to honor and toast the Moon Goddess and/or God that you were in rapport with during the Moon Sex Magick ritual.

13. Close the circle and put everything away. If you like, you can leave the circle open for moonbathing, which is lying skyclad in the full moon while meditating. Leaving the circle open overnight can also facilitate divine dreams.

Above all, be creative and have fun. I have provided love and sex magick methods that can adapted to each situation, whether prac-ticing solo, as a couple, or with more than two people, depending upon your sexual preference. Mixing and blending pantheons of Goddesses and Gods in ritual, like placing the symbols of Kerrid-wen, Isis, and Quan Yin together on your altar, is perfectly accept-able and I encourage you to do so.

Make an effort to incorporate the powerful elements of earth, air, fire, water, and spirit, which can be used to amplify and focus magickal energy. Whenever you are engaging in sex magick, be aware of the lunar, solar, and universal energies that are present.

Everything is energy. Love, sex, and magick reflect and utilize the polarities of this energy. By using love and sex magick, you can focus and direct the awesome amount of energy that stems from love and lovemaking toward your relationship, career, and spiritual patterns. This experience expands your body, mind, and spiritual awareness, and leads to a more fulfilling sex life, as you get in touch with your sexuality.

The thoughts, actions, and patterns into which you focus and direct your energy are the ones that will come to fruition. Whatever you turn your mind to, you give energy to. Random factors and unforeseen events sometimes occur, but as long as you are flexible, open to change, and willing to pivot you will be able to continue to work toward your patterns with the intention of actualizing your deepest dreams. Hopefully, the information and methods in this book will be of use to you today and in the years to come.

SOURCE DIRECTORY

All One Tribe Drum, (800) 442-DRUM; web site: www.allone-tribedrum.com
   Handmade and hand-painted drums, rattles, and accessories.

Ancient Circles, (800) 726-8032; web site: www.pacific.net/-ancient
   Fine Celtic jewelry.

Astral Seas, (800) 732-1734
   Handcrafted incense and oils, specialty items such as bath salts and soaps. Custom Celtic or ancestral labeling and packaging available.

Aureus, (800) 459-8463
   Fine incense and oils.

Azure Green/Abyss Distribution, (413) 623-2155
   Incense, scrying mirrors, candles, gifts, ritual items, cards, jewelry, books, tarot decks, talismans, and more.

Brigid's Fire, (800) 815-FIRE
   Symbolic Celtic jewelry.

Central Casting, (800) 745-1350
   Amulets, animal spirits, rune stones, and sacred goddesses.

Cheryl Briggs, (800) 548-5223
   Celtic pendants, ritual chalices, wands, and custom work.

Coyote Found Candles, (800) 788-4142
   Beeswax, plant vegetable, and standard candles. One of the best places to purchase your candles. Source for beeswax candles in the

shape of the Goddess, beeswax kits, and prism candles in rainbow colors.

Crystal Courier Import, Inc., (800) 397-1863
Incense, wands, runes, crystals, and gemstones.

Damel Studio Ltd., (800) 89-DAMEL
Statuary and wall hangings of Celtic Goddesses and Faeries.

Deva Designs, (800) 799-8308
Goddess figurines, totem pendants, and Goddess figures.

Dryad Design, (800) 392-7705
Original designs by Paul Borda, Celtic Goddess statues (Rhiannon, Kerridwen, and the Morrigan).

Earth Scents, (800) 933-5267
Oils, incense, and aromatherapy.

Fellowship Foundry Pewtersmiths, (510) 352-0935
Pewter chalices, ritual tools, jewelry, handfasting cups, chalices, statues, and accessories.

Feng Shui 2000, (423) 870-5699; web site: www.fs2000.com
Feng shui supplies and accessories.

Heaven and Earth, (800) 942-9423
Metaphysical jewelry, gems, minerals, crystals, and books.

JBL Devotional Statues, (800) 290-6203; web site: www.jblstatue.com/
Many Celtic Goddess and God statues for altar and display.

Karen's Fine Art Products, (818) 798-9307
Celtic Goddess and fairy ornaments, cards, boxes, bookmarks, and decorative ceramic tiles.

Lost Mountain Trading Company, (800) 800-6319; E-mail: lostmntn@coolstones.com
Rune stones carved into semiprecious gemstones such as hematite, amethyst, citrine, and rose quartz; rune pendants; Celtic jewelry; Celtic rings for handfasting.

McNamara's Green, (206) 523-0306
Celtic music, pagan books, Celtic jewelry, and more.

Nancy B. Watson's Potions, (800) 380-1080
Magick potions, salts, waters, and sands.

Open Circle Distributors, (800) 726-8032; E-mail: ancient@pacific.net
Celtic jewelry, scarves, and bags.

The Pendulum Works!, (800) 915-1151; E-mail: andras@sedona.net
Crystals, gemstones, crystal and gemstone pendulums, silk and cloth
pouches, beaded mojo bags.

Sacred Alchemy, (800) 522-0895
Pure essential ritual and healing oils with crystals.

Salem West, (614) 421-7557; web site: www.neopagan.com
Complete store of pagan supplies and books. Ritual tools, herbs,
jewelry, statues, masks, incense burners, drums, crystals, gemstones,
custom-made ritual tools, jewelry, and ceramics.

Shabda, (800) 678-3013
Incense, amber charms, candles, and Celtic jewelry.

Shiva Imports, (800) 368-4238
Incense, crystals, jewelry, Egyptian beads, singing bowls, boxes, and
Buddhist statues.

Sorcerer's Apprentice, (608) 271-7591
Silk robes, altar cloths, incense, and gemstones.

Strung-Out-and-Stoned Gems, (800) 72-ROCKS
Pentacles, knotwork, circles, and spirals.

Sun's Eye, (800) SUNS EYE (786-7393)
Mystical and magickal oils, bath salts, and candles. E-mail:
sunseye@iag.net

Visabella, (800) 474-9567
Fine quality velvet ritual gowns and hooded capes.

Waterhawk Creations, (216) 666-8745
Boxes, pendants, ritual tools, and one-of-a-kind pieces.

The Wax House, (888) WAX-9711; web site: www.waxhouse.com
Candle-making supplies, beeswax sheets in every color of the rainbow, molds, and candle oils.

Wellstone, (800) 544-8773
Fine jewelry in sterling silver or fourteen-karat gold, symbols of
Herne, the Green Man, spirals, torcs, and moons available. Images
with and without gemstones.

Whispered Prayers, (530) 894-2927; web site: www.whispered prayers.com

A huge variety of pagan supplies and books. Incense, smudge, altar tiles, jewelry, candles, ritual tools, oils, herbs, scrying mirrors, robes, crystals, and gemstones.

White Light Pentacles/Sacred Spirit Products, (800) MASTERY

Ritual tools, crystals, incense, runes, talismans, candles, and jewelry.

WindRose Trading Co., Inc., (800) 229-3731

Incense, incense holders, rolled Tibetan incense, diffusers, stone statues, perfume oils, and hand-painted rainbow silk bags.

Z Productions, (972) 438-2072

Robes, capes with Celtic trim, and ritual tools and cloths, many with Celtic designs.

GLOSSARY

AMULET   An object traditionally made of metal or stone that has feelings or effects placed in it. Often carried, or worn as a ring or as a necklace.

ARCHETYPES   Symbolic representations of universal principles, defining concepts in a symbolic form.

ATHAME   A ceremonial knife, two-sided by tradition, but now sometimes one-sided, representing the fire element.

BA-GUA   The eight-sided energetic overlay based on the energetics of the eight directions, Chinese I Ching trigrams, and a front-door location. The eight sides of the Ba-Gua are career, knowledge, family/health, wealth, fame, marriage, children/creativity, and helpful people/travel.

BELTANE   The beginning of May, or May 1. Also known as Bel Fire (*Bel* meaning "bright"), and the Adventure of the Sun.

BOUNDLESS   A vast and infinite place of being. Oneness.

BOWL   Craft tool used for salt and water or earth.

BRIDGET'S FIRE   The second Great Day, following Yule.

CANDLE   Represents the fire element in magickal works.

CANDLESTICK   Craft tool used on altar. Customarily three candlesticks with three candles (green–left side of altar, red–right side of altar, white–at the center).

CELTS   The ancient Gauls and Britons. Welsh, Irish, Highland Scots, Manx, Cornish, and Breton peoples of central and western Europe.

CHAKRAS   Wheels of energy located up and down our bodies. There are seven basic chakras from the base of the spine upward to the top of the head: root or base, sacral (below the navel), solar plexus, heart, throat, third eye, and crown.

CHALICE   A loving cup traditionally made of metal or clay. A consecrated tool symbolizing the water element and the concept of Oneness.

CHI   The energy flow that permeates and connects all things.

CIRCLE   Sacred light space constructed by the practitioner for magickal work. Also refers to the Family of the Tuatha.

CONCEPT OF ONENESS   Foundation of Druid tradition saying that all things are one, whatsoever they may be.

CONDITIONING   State of being that reflects the culmination of one's ancestry, upbringing, experience, personality, and culture. Not the true self, but a somewhat practical collection of valences and reactions that an individual wears as a way to maneuver in the world.

CRAFT TOOLS   Consecrated objects used to aid the practitioner in merging: athame, chalice, wand, robe, cord, incense burner, candlestick, and bowl.

CUTTING FIELDS   Disrupting or harmful energy fields, often unhealthy and considered unlucky.

DAYS OF POWER   The Eight Great Days and thirteen High Moons of ritual celebration.

DIVINATION   The art and science of forecasting or reading events using tools such as oghams, runes, and tarot cards.

EIGHT-SPOKED WHEEL   The wheel of the sun, which includes the Eight Great Days. Each spoke denotes one of these days.

ELEMENTS   Four traditional elements, often a fifth. Fire, earth, air, and water. The fifth element is the practitioner, or spirit.

FEMALE ENERGY   The Goddess represented by the color green and associated with the left side, the state of being receptive, and dreaming.

FENG SHUI   Means "the way of the wind and water." The primary concept of feng shui is to work in harmony with the elements and natural energy flows, thus transforming negative sha into positive chi through various cures.

FOUR WARDS   The four corners of North, East, South and West. Also called the Watchtowers or the Great Wards.

GEM ESSENCE   A healing or spiritual tincture or elixir made from gemstones and a liquid such as water or wine.

GOD   Male energy, male archetype. A being in a merged state. Father God.

GODDESS   Female energy, female archetype. A being in a merged state. Mother Goddess.

HELLITH'S DAY   The seventh Great Day, usually celebrating the harvest, which takes place on the Autumn Equinox.

HIGH MOONS   The twelve or thirteen full moons in a yearly cycle. Starting with the first full moon after Yule, they are the Wolf, Storm, Chaste, Seed, Hare, Dyad, Mead, Wort, Barley, Wine, Blood, Snow, and Oak. A time of healing rituals and for dreaming.

KAMA SUTRA   The classical Indian text on eroticism, means "to sew love."

KUNDALINI   The energy that rests at the base of your spine or root chakra that waits to be awakened. When awakened, the energy moves up your chakras into your crown chakra, which is symbolic of the mating of the Goddess Shakti and the God Shiva.

LADY'S DAY   Also called Hertha's Day. The third Great Day of the cycle, traditionally associated with the beginning of Spring.

LETHA'S DAY   The sixth Great day of the cycle, also called Midsummer.

LUGHNASSAD   The seventh Great Day, which takes place in August. Lugh's wedding feast. Considered the time when the forces of light and dark converge, and the sun and moon are equal.

MAGICK   The study of the nature of all things. The use of ritual to continue the cycle of the Goddess and God.

MAGICKAL ARTS   Patterning and building patterns with intention, expectation, desire, and merging.

MALE ENERGY   The consort represented by the color red and associated with the right side, the state of emitting, and doing.

MERGING   The state of becoming one with all things. Diffusing into the boundless, into Oneness.

NEGATIVITY   A destructive energetic force that breaks patterns and feeds upon itself. Moving counterclockwise. Associated with the Dark One.

ONENESS   The boundless. A place where one is connected to all things and to nothing.

PATTERNS   A term for discussing one's intentions and expectations. The formula and foundation from which one merges and experiences all things.

POSITIVITY   An energetic force that creates and builds energy and patterns. Associated with the Bright One.

PRACTITIONER   A person who practices magick.

QUARTZ CRYSTAL   Quartz that is almost transparent to completely transparent.

RAPPORT   Harmony of relationship with another, to be in close accord. Remembering who we really are and understanding the deeper connection.

ROBE   Your sacred and magickal skin.

RUNNING THE LIGHT   Moving mass amounts of energy during a magickal work or with a sexual partner during lovemaking.

SACRED MARRIAGE   Spiritual union with the Goddess and God. You become the Goddess and God.

SAMHAIN   All Hallows' Eve and the eighth Great Day, associated with death and rebirth. The day when the veil between time and space is the thinnest.

SEX MAGICK   The sexual and magickal practice of using sexual intercourse to generate, direct, and release vast amounts of energy toward specific goals.

SHA   Negative energy flow.

SPIRITUAL PARTNERSHIP   A sacred bond between two people.

SUNWISE   Clockwise turning, which is considered the positive direction; builds energy. The opposite of widdershins, or counterclockwise.

SYMBOLS   The representation of many things in one thing.

TANTRA   The sacred sexual practice originating in the East.

TAROT CARDS   A divination tool using archetypal and symbolic visual representations.

THIRD EYE   The sixth chakra, a point between the eyes and above the nose. Thought to be where psychic ability and clairvoyance reside.

THREE EYES OF KERRIDWEN   The formula for magickal works consisting of intention and expectation, desire, and merging.

THREE SECRETS REINFORCEMENT   1. mudra, which is what you do with your hands: left hand over the right and thumbs joined at forty-five degrees; 2. manta, which is the saying, OM, MA, NI, PAD, ME, HUM, repeated nine times in each of the corners and center of the Ba-Gua; and 3. creative visualization.

APPENDIX A

LOVE AND SEX CANDLE MAGICK

Using candle magick always enhances love, sex, and magickal practices. Be aware of the time of day, moon phases, and astrological influences when doing candle magick and rituals. Candle magick can be as simple as dedicating a candle to a special God or Goddess, or it can be the main focal point in ritual, with many other components added, for instance, crystals and gemstones, scented oils, incense, items from nature, herbs, flowers, resins, and so forth.

When doing candle magick, candles should be allowed to burn down completely. Then bury or discard the candle appropriately. If you need to put out the candle, do so with wetted fingers or a snuffer. The instructions in this appendix are intended as a guideline for your candle-magick rituals. Be creative and use your intuition.

Candle Colors

WHITE   Goddess or God rapport, divine power and protection, divine inspiration, purity, positive motivation.

RED   love, lust, sexual energy, vitality, physical strength, courage, dynamic creativity, action.

GREEN   healing, natural growth, new growth, nature, abundance, fertility, good luck, harmony, money, dreaming, shapeshifting.

BLUE   cleansing, clearing blockages, higher wisdom, inspiration, washing away negativity, psychic protection.

YELLOW/GOLD   power, communication, mental awareness, knowledge, protection, mental creativity, sun rapport.

SILVER   dreaming, moon rapport, ancestor communication, clairvoyance and telepathy, astral travel, channeling.

PURPLE/VIOLET   psychic ability and awareness, spiritual power, higher wisdom, channeling deity, dimensional communication.

PINK   love, friendship, romance, playfulness, healing emotions, relationships, family ties, children.

ORANGE   healing the body, meditation, higher wisdom, positive energy, fair play.

BLACK   protection, getting rid of negativity, ending negative relationships, tapping into the deep unconscious, working with the shadow self.

Four Corners, Elements, and Correspondences

NORTH   (earth) ancestors, divinity, Gods and Goddesses.

EAST   (air) patterns, mastery, thoughts, ideas.

SOUTH   (fire) creative rire, power, change, transformation.

WEST   (water) emotions, feelings, flow, intuition.

Dressing Your Candle

1. Wash and rinse the candle(s) in salt water.
2. Carve any names, initials, and symbols (three times) on the candle with a regular writing pen, your athame, a quill, or a pointed stick.
3. Apply magickal oils to the candle, covering it completely with a thin coat of scented oil.
4. Crystals and gemstones are especially effective components in candle magick. Place tumbled gemstones around your candle in a circle, heart, or medicine wheel configuration, or use

clear crystal points to create a crystal grid around your candle. To create a simple grid, place four crystals at each of the four directions, pointing toward the candle. Please refer to Appendix D: Love, Sex, and Magick Crystals and Gemstones for detailed information on the magickal uses of crystals and stones.

5. Add herbs and flowers to your candle-magick circle, sprinkling them inside the crystal circle or grid. See Appendix C: Love, Sex, and Magick Herbs, Flowers, and Resins for properties and uses.

Thirteen Steps to Candle Magick

1. Set up your altar. Dress your candle as discussed in steps 1 to 5 above, and set it on your altar.
2. Draw a sacred circle.
3. Establish the direction corners, North, East, South, and West, and clear them.
4. Call in the Four Wards and elements.
5. Select a Sponsor God and/or Goddess. Choose the Goddess or God you feel the strongest rapport with. Ask them to help you in your candle-magick ritual.
6. Choose a sponsor power animal, selecting an animal you have no fear of, and ask them to help you in your magickal work.
7. Create a simple chant or song, saying specifically what it is that you want to achieve with your candle-magick ritual. Include the names of any sponsor deities and power animals.
8. Light the candle with care.
9. Merge with the flame of the candle and connect with the divine energy—Goddess and God. Do this for at least fifteen minutes. Use deep breathing to intensify your focus and connection.
10. Allow the candle to burn down completely. If you leave the

room, be sure the candle is positioned where it can burn down safely without being disturbed.

11. Bury or discard the candle appropriately.
12. Clean up and put everything away.
13. Burn incense or smudge, or scatter salt to clear and purify your ritual area, and/or take a magickal bath.

(Please refer to Chapter 5 for complete instructions for setting up your altar, drawing the sacred circle, establishing the corners, and calling in the Wards.)

Candle Magick Rituals

Pink Candle-Magick Ritual for Love and Friendship

OIL   mint, lemon, orange, strawberry, clove, or coconut.

GEMSTONES   rose quartz and amethyst in a circle.

FRESH OR DRIED FLOWERS AND HERBS   lavender, jasmine, passion flower, chamomile.

DEDICATION   Bridget, Angus Og, Manannan, Caer, Eros, Aphrodite, Isis, Shakti, Kama, Shiva, Krishna, Psyche, Edain, Halcyone, Hero, and others.

Red Candle-Magick Ritual for Sexual Empowerment and Lust

OIL   vanilla, patchouli, ylang-ylang, sandalwood, or amber.

GEMSTONES   Stones placed at the four corners: green (North), clear or gold (East), red, orange, or rutile (South), blue or aqua (West).

FRESH OR DRIED FLOWERS AND HERBS   rose petals, apple, sunflowers, patchouli, poppy, peach, cinnamon, ginseng, rosemary.

DEDICATION   Anu, Dagda, Math, Lugh, Viviana, Rosemerta, Dwyn, Angus Og, Boann, Kama, Shakti, Krishna, Shiva, Flora, Freya, Hathor, Ishtar, Sheila na Gig, Anna Perenna, Artemis, Helen, and others.

White Candle-Magick for Divine Love

OIL   lavender, narcissus, amber, gardenia, or lotus.

GEMSTONES   three tumbled clear quartz or rutile stones positioned in a triangle, or three clear quartz points that are pointed in toward the candle.

FRESH OR DRIED FLOWERS AND HERBS   bay, lily, daisy, pine, mistletoe, rosebuds, jasmine, orchid.

DEDICATION   Kerridwen, Kernunnos, Branwen, Math, Anu, Gwydion, Taliesin, Bridget, Jesus, Buddha, Kama, Isis, Odin, Enki, Krishna, Ra, Oshun, Venus, and others.

APPENDIX B
LOVE, SEX, AND MAGICK OILS

Each concentrated essence or a plant represents the spirit of the plant and is the carrier of its energy and qualities. Plants absorb energies from the sun, moon, and earth, storing this vital life force that can be tapped and used in magick. You can release the power of oils by wearing them, as the heat of your body releases the scent. Be aware that some oils can irritate your skin. I suggest you test each oil on a tiny patch of soft skin inside your arm, for example, before using it in your bath water or in massage oil. If you have any negative reaction, discontinue use.

If wearing certain oils irritates your skin, an option is to place a drop or two on a cotton ball and carry it in your pocket and then burn the oils in incense, or if you are sensitive to smoke, by using an infuser. Putting a few drops in a small pan of boiling water also releases the powerful and magickal fragrances of oils.

Suggestions for using scented oils include always wearing the same scent whenever you are with your prospective mate. In certain situations, use other scents to layer your primary scent. For example, wear amber-scented oil on your body and use lavender-scented oil in your bedroom. Your mate then identifies amber oil with you and lavender oil with your bedroom. You can then use your personal scent to immediately influence your personal space, creating a kind of magickal state induced by your fragrance. You can also use your personal scent on paper and envelopes, and every note you write and every gift you give your lover.

Love Oil Blend: One-half cup of almond oil, nine petals from one red or pink rose, one teaspoon of dried basil, one teaspoon of dried marjoram. For the scent to grow stronger, let these ingredients steep together in a dark bottle for several days. Do not use the leafy parts of flowers.

Basic Formula for Preparing Oils

First, you need to obtain a carrier oil. I prefer edible oils such as almond or extra-lite olive oil. Jojoba oil also works well. Use only fresh oil. Add a few drops of wheat germ oil as a preservative if you find your oils do not keep well.

The basic fragrance oil formula is simple. First put the crushed herb, flowers, or resin in a bottle of oil. Roll the bottle between the palms of your hands for about ten minutes, until the oil is warm. Store the bottle in a dark place and wait until the fragrance is to your liking. Usually a couple of weeks to three months should be enough time for the oils to age and become fragrant. I find that resins such as amber work best in oils when you use tiny pieces of the resin because the pieces float to the bottom. Then, as the oil ages, it becomes more potent.

If you don't want herbs or flowers in your finished oils, use the foot of a nylon sock, muslin, or cheesecloth to put the herbs or flowers in and suspend them by a string into a wide-mouthed bottle. Or you can strain the oil through a wire mesh sieve. (A tea sieve works well for this purpose.) When left in the oil some herbs will cause the oil to go stale, so I suggest straining your finished products if you plan on keeping them for more than a few weeks.

If you use oils on your skin, be sure to test a patch of skin by applying a few drops to see if the oil irritates you or causes allergic reactions.

The best bottles in which to store your oils are sterilized dark brown bottles with a dropper top. I save all of my brown herbal tincture bottles just for the purpose of storing essential oils. Be sure to label the bottle with the date, the type of oil it contains, and your formula.

Following is a list of oils and their magickal uses:

ACACIA   Protection, love, blessing, and psychic powers.

ALLSPICE   Money, luck, healing, and the belly chakra.

ALMOND   Prosperity and wisdom.

AMBER   Love, happiness, and strength.

APPLE BLOSSOM   Love, happiness, and uplifting.

APRICOT   Love, creativity, and mental openness.

ASTER   Unconditional love.

BALSAM, FIR   Prosperity and mental clarity.

BAY   Attracts women, calms nerves, enhances psychic powers, and protects against negativity.

BAYBERRY   Money, prosperity, energy, and clarity.

BENZOIN   Purification, prosperity; a divine rapport, and balance.

BIRCH   Protection, purification, cooling, and soothing emotions.

CAMELLIA   Prosperity and gentleness.

CAMPHOR   Divination and clarity.

CARNATION   Protection, blessing; stimulates and strengthens.

CEDAR   Money, healing, protection, purification, calming, comforting, and strengthening.

CHAMOMILE   Money, love, purification; calming and relaxing.

CHERRY   Love and divination.

CHERRY BLOSSOM   Peace, harmony, happiness, and balancing.

CINNAMON   Psychic powers, protection, love-power; stimulates creativity and acts as an antidepressant.

CITRUS   Psychic powers, healing, clarity, and mental focus.

CLOVER   Protection, prosperity, love-fidelity, and an antidepressant.

CLOVES   Protection, prosperity, purification, love, and mental powers.

COCONUT   Love, courage, protection, and inner peace.

CUMIN   Protection, exorcism, love-fidelity; dispels negativity.

DRAGON'S BLOOD   Love, protection, exorcism, crown chakra, and control of energies.

FRANGIPANI   Magnetizing, attracts opposite sex, love, and stimulates the heart and base chakra.

FRANKINCENSE   Protection, exorcism; purifies, uplifts, and strengthens.

GARDENIA   Love-peace, spirituality, and stimulation of the heart chakra.

GERANIUM   Love-fertility, protection, calming, balancing, and an antidepressant.

GINGER   Prosperity, love, power, healing; strengthens and warms the spirit.

GINGER BLOSSOM   Love, passion, healing, warms the spirit, and is used for the root chakra, as it activates and fires up the lower chakra.

GINSENG   Love, beauty-passion, healing-vitality, inner radiance.

GRAPE   Prosperity, fertility, and mental clarity.

HIBISCUS   Love, passion, divination, and the union of the upper and lower chakras.

HONEY   Love, prosperity; calms, relaxes, and balances.

HONEYSUCKLE   Prosperity, protection, and psychic powers; relaxing, soothing, and uplifting.

HYACINTH   Love, happiness, protection, and optimism.

JASMINE   Love-money, dreams, spiritual love and raising vibrations; an antidepressant and aphrodisiac.

JUNIPER   Purification, protection, love, centering; strengthens; an antidepressant.

LAVENDER   Love-peace, purification, protection; calming, balancing, strengthening, and stimulating.

LEMON   Purification, love, friendship, clarity; calms and helps mental powers.

LEMON GRASS   Psychic powers, passion; a tonic, refreshing.

LEMON-LIME   Purification, love, friendship, clarity, mental powers; calming.

LILAC   Exorcism, protection, peace-harmony, mind clearing; aids memory and concentration.

LIME   Enhances friendship, strengthens and stimulates the body, acts as an antidepressant.

LOTUS   Protection, relaxing and cooling.

MAGNOLIA   Love-fidelity, purity, and clear thinking.

MANDRAKE   Protection, love-fertility, prosperity; control of spiritual energies and power.

MARJORAM   Protection, love-happiness, prosperity, relieves nervous tension and exhaustion.

MINT   Passion, protection, travel, exorcism, clarity; increases memory and concentration, refreshing,.

MISTLETOE   Protection, exorcism, love-fertility; dispels negativity.

MUGWORT   Astral travel, prophetic dreams, and psychic powers.

MUSK   Enhances personality, determination, and strengthens focus.

MYRRH   Protection, exorcism, spirituality; cools emotions, balances, stimulates the third eye and crown chakra.

NARCISSUS   Divination, strengthens connection with other planes.

NUTMEG   Luck, prosperity, fidelity; increases dreams, strengthens, and calms

ORANGE   Love, prosperity, divination; luck, relaxation, balancing; stimulating and sensual.

ORANGE BLOSSOM   Love, magnetic attraction, success, compelling, persuasion; calming, relaxing, an antidepressant; stimulates belly and heart chakras.

ORANGE MANDARIN   Happiness, joy, calming, relaxing; an antidepressant.

ORCHID   Love, inner beauty, and harmony.

PAPAYA   Love, protection, and intuition.

PASSION FLOWER   Friendship and peace.

PATCHOULI   Prosperity, passion-fertility; an aphrodisiac.

PEACH   Love-fertility, exorcism, wishes-luck; dispels negativity and strengthens connections with higher spirits.

PEPPERMINT   Purification, psychic powers, healing, and mental clarity; an antidepressant.

PINE   Fertility, prosperity, exorcism, protection, strengthening; cleansing and regenerative.

POPPY   Sleep, love-fertility, luck, invisibility, intuition, and prophetic dreams.

PRIMROSE   Protection, love, unconditional love, and spirituality.

RASPBERRY   Protection, love, optimism, brightness, and clarity.

ROSE   Love, luck, divination protection, peace, balancing; strengthens the heart chakra and spirit.

ROSEMARY   Protection, love-passion, mental powers, purification, uplifting, a mental stimulant, builds strength of character and courage.

SAFFRON   Love-passion, happiness, psychic powers.

SAGE   Wisdom, protection, purification; cleanses, balances, and strengthens.

SANDALWOOD   Protection, exorcism, spirituality, and harmony.

SESAME   Prosperity, passion, and root and heart chakra.

SPEARMINT   Love, mental powers, and inner clarity.

STRAWBERRY   Love, luck, and joy.

SWEET PEA   Love-friendship, courage, strength, loyalty, and devotion; compelling-drawing.

THYME   Health, courage, purification, love; strengthens.

TULIP   Prosperity, love, protection, and awareness of the earth spirit.

VANILLA   Passion, mental powers; calms, soothes nerves, and relaxes.

VERBENA   Prosperity, love-peace, protection, and purification; calms and improves concentration.

VIOLET   Soothes the nerves, encourages passion, used in love charms, stimulates throat-chakra healing and the heart center.

YLANG-YLANG   Used for strengthening and balancing your energy, as an aphrodisiac, and to attract higher vibrations of energy.

Appendix C

LOVE, SEX, AND MAGICK HERBS, FLOWERS, AND RESINS

Growing and Using Herbs

Avoid using any metal garden implements (especially iron), cooking pots, utensils, or containers in all herbal processes, except incense. Pay close attention to the tools you use when boiling the water for your herbal preparations, using only glass and ceramic cooking pans. Also, be especially aware of your intention as you handle the herbs.

Be aware that location, climate, and season influence herbal properties. Rituals can be observed in growing, harvesting, and using mother nature's sacred gifts. Some say the dark of the moon or Midsummer's Eve are optimum times for gathering herbs. Take no more than one-third of the foliage of a plant, and only bits and pieces of bark from trees. Always treat plants with respect, thanking them for their natural gifts.

You are already familiar with the benefits of fresh herbs if you grow your own. I would encourage everyone to begin to grow and use herbs, thereby cultivating a healthy connection to nature. Consider the practical and magickal aspects of the adventure—space, soil, growing, harvesting, and collecting the seeds for the next year. You will be generously rewarded, as fresh herbs have incredible flavor, aroma, and endless uses.

Disclaimer/Warning

Herbs are potent remedies, and some herbs are poisonous. Remember to exercise caution when using herbs. They are effective in eliminating, detoxifying, maintaining, and building energies. To treat an illness or disease, or if you are pregnant, consult a knowledgeable professional—herbalist, acupuncturist, naturopathic, or homeopathic doctor—before beginning herbal therapy. Good herbal books are *The Way of Herbs,* by Michael Tierra, *The Medicine Grove,* by Loren Cruden, *An Elder's Herbal,* by David Hoffman, *The Fragrant Mind,* by Valerie Worwood, and *Essential Energy,* by Nikki Goldstein. Be sure to do a patch test if you are going to be using the herb on your skin or in your bath water.

Used properly, herbs can be safe and without side effects. Realize that herbal treatment will be gentle and gradual, allowing the body to heal itself, and that children are very sensitive to the energy of plants. With younger persons always use much smaller doses, under the supervision of a health-care professional.

Ways of Using Herbs, Flowers, and Resins

BATHS spread the herb's qualities over the body. Prepare your herbal bath by dropping an herbal sachet or infusion into the warm water.

DECOCTION uses the harder parts of herbs, like stems, bark, and roots. Simmer for ten to twenty minutes, until one-third of the water or liquid has decreased. Strain and use.

ESSENTIAL OILS are concentrated essences from aromatic herbs and plants, primarily used in aromatherapy. They are created by extracting herbal oils through steam distillation. Oils are worn on your skin or clothes, rubbed onto the surfaces of objects, dabbed onto sachets, added to baths, and burned as incense. Oils are very potent. Be aware that they may cause adverse reactions when applied directly to your skin.

EXTRACTS are highly concentrated forms of herbs and flowers in an alcohol base. Some extracts are available in nonalcohol forms. This is an easy way to add herbs to tea and baths.

INCENSE was common in ancient cultures and considered a sacred art. Vedic Rishis (the holy men in Hindu mythology) discovered that each herbal fragrance, like each color and sound, possessed a unique quality with the power to produce an altered state of consciousness. The first incenses were made from aromatic gums and resins. Today, incense is made from one herb or resin, or a mixture of herbs, flowers, and resins that are burned or smoldered on charcoal. You can burn the herbs after they have dried, or you can use a mortar and pestle to powder the herbs and then sprinkle them on the charcoal. Use a fireproof incense burner and take necessary precautions.

Be sure you have all of the ingredients you will need for the incense formula. Then grind each ingredient into a powder, using a mortar and pestle or an electric grinder. Most resins don't powder easily and gum up a bit when you first blend them. If you like, you can use loose herbs, flowers, and small pieces of resin applied directly to the burning charcoal disk, but you will find that powdered incenses burn and store much better.

When you are making the incense, focus on each ingredient, one at a time. Fix your mind on how the incense is going to be used, for example, in a love-magick ritual or love spell. Then, in a wooden, ceramic, or glass bowl, mix the ingredients together. A rule of thumb is to mix the resins and gums, then the dried herbs, flowers, barks, and roots, and finally add the oils. You can always use an oil for an herb or flower if there are enough dry ingredients in the formula. I recommend you use natural essential oils in your incense formulas. Once the incense is completely compounded, burn it and store any extra in a capped jar, labeled and dated.

For specific love, sex, and magick incense formulas, see Appendix G.

INFUSION describes a simple process of soaking herbs in hot water. Keep the infusion covered so the steam stays within the container. Using one teaspoon of herb to every cup of liquid, heat the water until boiling and pour it over the herb. Cover and let it steep several minutes. Then strain and let the liquid cool. One ounce of herbs to one pint of liquid can be used for medicinal teas. Infusions are also used in baths, rubbed on the body, or onto spiritual tools, altar tables, jewelry, furniture, and floors.

OINTMENT combines vegetable shortening or cocoa butter with herbs. Blend one cup shortening or butter to three tablespoons of powdered herbs. Mix them and store in an airtight container in a cool place. You can also melt the shortening and add a few drops of essential oil and then cool. Anoint your body at pulse points— both sides of the neck below your ears, the inside surface of your wrists, ankles, and the back of your head. The heart and third eye are optional anointing points.

SACHETS are small bags or pieces of natural cloth filled with herbs, used for carrying herbs in your pocket, purse, or tied in a bag around your neck. Household sachets are larger and placed in rooms to spread the scent and properties of the herbs throughout the area.

You can purchase sachet bags from metaphysical shops and health food stores or make your own by sewing together natural strips of cloth (3″ × 3″ or larger). Leave one end open to insert the herbs, and then sew or tie the end closed. If the herbs you are using are finely ground, use a very tight stitch setting when using a sewing machine. In a pinch, a knee-high nylon sock or regular sock, filled with herbs and then knotted on the end, also work as sachets.

Listing of Herbs, Flowers, and Resins

AMBER   A resin of the Goddess used in merging and ritual. Use amber essential oil on the third eye, behind the ears, wrists, ankles, and the back of the head to open the doorway between dimensions. Excellent for protection and often used in amulets. Attracts nature energies and beings to you, and enhances sex magick.

ANGELICA (AMERICAN AND EUROPEAN SPECIES), MASTERWORT   This herb warms the body and improves circulation, acting as an overall tonic and blood purifier for the body. Used in incense, scattered over your ritual space, carried on your person, or in infusions to enhance creative visions. Place angelica sachets in your bath to purify your mind and energy, setting the stage for clearer and stronger personal vision. (Should not be used by pregnant women or diabetics, either internally or on the skin).

APPLE   Fruit of the Goddess. Associated with the water element. The apple is the fruit of immortality and vitality. The apple branch, or Silver Branch, allows the practitioner to enter the Otherworld. Eating apples has long been known to prevent illness. Apples can also be used as poppets in love magick. Throwing apples is a sign of love, conveying fertility.

BARLEY   Associated with the Goddess and the earth element. Scattering barley clears negative energy in a magickal space. Barley is also used in magickal brews and potions, and eating barley soothes the internal body system. The Barley Mother is the Harvest Queen.

BURDOCK   Gathering on the waning or new moon makes the herb strongest. It purifies the body, balances, and equalizes. Burdock is used as an incense for protection from negativity.

BAY   Laurel. A masculine fire herb used for protection, psychic development, and magickal strength. Inhaling the scent of a fresh bay leaf gives you psychic clarity and prophetic dreams. Bay is used in brews and burned in incense, and is used in rituals as a purifier.

BEE POLLEN   Called the miracle food, bee pollen is one of the most complete energy foods, with its healing and rejuvenating properties. Oxygenates brain cells and increases endurance and strength. It also increases personal energy and memory.

BENZOIN   Excellent for balancing polarities such as female and male energies. Used for purification, consecration, and ritual. Attracts sacred and divine love.

BLESSED THISTLE   Our Lady's Thistle. As the national flower of Scotland, this herb strengthens memory and mental capacity. Aids circulation and vitality, and acts as an overall tonic for body, mind, and spirit. Thistle creates positive energy by diffusing negativity. It is used in baths to purify your personal energy field and connect you with your higher self and Oneness. Strong and tall thistle are used as magickal walking sticks.

CATNIP   Catmint, or cat's wort. Benefiting the mind by quieting the nervous system, catnip relaxes and promotes a more positive perspective. It soothes the nerves that are a result of built-up emotional tension and cultivates a feeling of love, beauty, and happiness by attracting positive energy. This is an excellent herb for children, used in combination with camomile, spearmint, and lemon balm as a tea. Sharing catnip with your feline friends will intoxicate them. Throughout history, large leaves of catnip were dried flat and used as bookmarks in metaphysical and magickal works.

CAYENNE   Capsicum. The fruit of a plant of the nightshade family, cayenne is considered a superior crisis herb. Often used in herbal combinations and known as a catalyst for all herbs, it increases circulation and acts as an excellent tonic for the nervous system. Used as an overall healing herb, cayenne is taken as a daily tonic and is nonirritating when uncooked. By drawing out impurities in your system, it normalizes blood pressure and relieves stress. This herb feeds the cell structure of arteries, veins, and capillaries so they will regain elasticity. Handle cooked cayenne with care, as it can be irritating to the mucous membranes and causes a warm sensation in the stomach, and even a burning sensation throughout your system. Natives in Central and South America used cayenne to cure disease.

CEDAR   Burned as incense, it purifies your magickal space. Cedar has strong tree energy and wisdom and is an herb of the sun. Good for head colds and is used in sweat baths.

CINNAMON   Associated with the sun. Powerful for love and sex magick and used to enhance psychic abilities and creativity. Mood elevator.

COPAL   A resin that is added to love incenses when burned over charcoal; associated with the purifying energy of fire and the powers of the sun.

CORIANDER   Used in love and sex magick. The powdered seed is used in potions and added to the chalice in ritual.

DAMIANA   Renews the energy in your body and acts as a sexual rejuvenator. This herb is worn, burned in incense, and carried to promote lust and passion. Place damiana in red sachets or vials to increase its power.

DANDELION   A herb of the air element, it is used for calling the Goddess and God. The roasted root used in tea is tasty and will promote magickal abilities and seeing. An herb that balances body energies.

DRAGON'S BLOOD   Blood, Draconis Resina, Blume. Used for love, potency, prowess, and protection. This resin is burned in incense to entice wayward lovers to return. Drives away negativity when sprinkled on the altar and around your home. A pinch of dragon's blood increases the power of all other incenses.

ECHINACEA   Coneflower. Used for strengthening all magickal and healing works. A multidimensional herb. A natural antibiotic and all-heal. Uses include relieving symptoms of colds, flus, and infections.

ENGLISH DAISY   Called bairnwort because children use this herb to make daisy chains. Used to make May Day crowns and an excellent flower to decorate your altar.

FENNEL   Associated with the masculine god and the fire element. Used for healing, protection, and purification. Soothes the stomach and digestive system. Use in sachets and healing mixtures.

FLAX   Linseed. An herb of fire and earth elements. The Goddess taught humankind how to cultivate flax and spin it into thread. Protects against any energetic attack and is used in healing mixtures. Sprinkle healing areas with flax seed.

FRANKINCENSE   A fragrant tree gum resin associated with fire, used to honor solar deities. Burned to set magickal space in place and used for protection, purification, and consecration. Induces merging and helps in meditation. Accelerates spiritual growth.

GARLIC   Stinkweed. Considered to be a cure-all by most cultures, garlic should not be boiled when used in herbal therapy, as this can take away its medicinal value. The fresh juice is most effective in reducing blood pressure, detoxifying and rejuvenating everything it comes in contact with inside and outside the body. The herb promotes cell growth and repair in healing. Garlic absorbs negativity and is used for protection and shielding, either worn on the body as an amulet or hung in the house. Aristotle mentioned using garlic for a spring tonic. Garlic was also eaten or laid at the crossroads to honor the Greek Goddess Hecate, the triple Goddess of the underworld who bestows wealth, success, advice, and good luck.

GINKO BILOBA   Improves mental clarity and capacity. Helps improve blood circulation to the brain, helping memory and reaction time. An effective herb for staying healthy and feeling younger with more energy.

GINSENG (American)   Wonder of the World root. Known as the king of all tonics, ginseng was used by Native Americans throughout history. To look upon the root gives strength and vigor. This herb assists in all mental activities, stimulating your entire body's energy, helping you overcome stress and fatigue. By nourishing the blood it increases the capillary circulation of the brain and enhances creativity on all levels. American ginseng is considered cooling and a summer tonic. Use the herb to draw positive energy toward you, or carry ginseng for beauty and harmony. (Persons with high blood pressure should avoid using ginseng unless recommended by an herbal professional).

GINSENG (Wild Siberian)   Regenerates and restores sexual centers. Anciently known as a male hormone and used for longevity. The Chinese say ginseng is a cure-all; it builds the body, both mental and physical, and is believed to slow the aging process.

GOLDEN SEAL   Used in healing rituals. A masculine herb favored by solar Goddesses and Gods. A natural antibiotic for infections, colds, and flus. Raises the metabolism rate and body temperature.

GOTU KOLA   Indian pennywort. Containing incredible rejuvenating properties, this herb is called the Secret of Perpetual Youth. It strengthens the heart, memory, and brain, stimulates circulation to the brain, and acts as a nerve tonic. Gotu kola is used to increase learning ability and promotes memory and mental clarity. It is one of the most widely used herbs in the Ayurvedic tradition (called Brahmi) and is known for increasing longevity. Gotu kola is traditionally burned before meditation.

HONEYSUCKLE   Woodbine. An herb used for magickal development and protection of patterns. When used on the third eye, it opens psychic ability. An essential oil used in consecrating tools and other magickal items. Also useful in merging and sex magick. Many pines have honeysuckle clinging to them. Honeysuckle, *uilleand* in Gaelic, is one of the family of sacred trees of the Ogham alphabet. The bird associated with honeysuckle is the lapwing.

JASMINE   The tea increases erotic feelings. Steep two teaspoons of jasmine flowers to each cup of water for about twenty minutes and drink a quarter cup, four times a day. Excellent herb for love and sex magick, candle magick, and for use in incense, sachets, and love charms. Attracts spiritual and sacred love. Add jasmine flowers to your ritual cup for love magick, or spread them clockwise around the edge of your sacred circle.

JUNIPER BERRIES   Associated with fire and the sun, excellent for purification, protection, and centering. Used for strengthening love magick.

LAVENDER   Cast into bonfires at Midsummer as a love offering to the Goddess and God, lavender becomes a potent ingredient in love and sex magic. The scent attracts men and promotes peace, joy, and a sense of well-being. Use for ritual anointing, in incense, baths, and sachets, and sprinkle inside your stones grids in candle magick.

LEMON   For love and friendship. Encourages insights while calming and quieting the mind.

LICORICE ROOT   Vitalizes the body and strengthens the circulatory system. Gives renewed vigor and sexual energy, and creates a warming sensation in your body. Licorice root is chewed to increase sexual energy and is added to love potions and used in sex magick rituals. Promotes fidelity and passion in sexual union.

LOTUS   A sacred and divine flower used in tantra, love, and sex magick. Has relaxing, soothing, and cooling properties.

MANDRAKE   Sorcerer's root. An herb used for protection, fertility, and abundance. Worn to protect against illness and used in image magick. Dried mandrake root can be activated by soaking it in warm water overnight. Place the root in water for one lunar cycle, new to full, and use it to sprinkle oils and herbs on your altar.

MARIGOLD   Bride of the sun. Used for protection, prophetic dreams, and magickal development. An herb for dreaming and strengthening second sight. A favorite of the faeries.

MARJORAM   Wintersweet. The most common herb in love and fertility spells, marjoram is woven into handfasting wreaths and added to food to strengthen desire. Marjoram can be used as a component in love potions, as it was sacred to Venus and Aphrodite. Carried and grown for protection, this herb helps to restore mental balance. Used for depression and colds.

MARSHMALLOW   Althea; sweet weed. Stimulates the mind and regulates the heat of the body. This herb is a good tonic for the entire body; it is especially high in minerals. About 10 percent of the marshmallow herb is used in teas, usually in combination with other herbs. As a blood purifier, it rids your body of toxins. A comforting and calming herb, marshmallow encourages healing, promoting cell growth and repair. Psychic abilities are enhanced, and the herb imparts positivity, ridding a place of negative influences. Acting as a spirit magnet, marshmallow strengthens your connection to Oneness and the spiritual aspects of the cosmos by pulling these energies to you. Used in sachets and burned as incense.

MEADOWSWEET   Queen of the meadow, bridewort, or bride's flower. One of the most sacred herbs of the Druids. Used in love spells and associated with the planet Jupiter. Its scent warms the heart and promotes passion and loving feelings. The flowers are usually included in the bridal bouquet.

MINT   (Spearmint) An herb of the God and the air element. Used in healing mixtures and potions. Good for headaches and the general well-being of the body. A stomach soother. Promotes sleep. Used together with marjoram and rosemary, mint rids an area of negativity. An herb of protection and for calling in the light beings of the Otherworld.

MISTLETOE   Golden bough, holy wood, birdlime. This herb was given to the keeping of the Goddess of Love and Fertility, and this is why people still kiss under its boughs. Used for amulets and wands. An herb of the sun, mistletoe offers strong protection and magickal power, enhances all magick, and is excellent for dreaming. Do not ingest the berries, wood, or leaves.

MUGWORT   An herb associated with the earth element, used for dreaming, protection, and astral travel, as well as psychic development and magickal strength. Used in potions and brews for divination.

MYRRH   A feminine moon resin used for protection, healing, and spiritual development. Myrrh is sacred to the Egyptian Goddess Isis. It is burned to purify magickal space, usually in conjunction with other resins. The smoke is used to consecrate magickal tools and assists in merging and healing works.

NETTLE   Stinging nettle. A masculine fire herb used for healing and protection. Aids in recovery, soothes skin and internal organs; natural palliative. Good for purification baths.

NO SHOU WU   A sexual tonic for generative energy and rejuvenating your entire body.

ORANGE   Excellent for divination, luck, prosperity, and balancing energies. Used to stimulate the senses in love and sex magick.

PASSION FLOWER   Passion vine, maypops. This herb has a calming effect, helps relieve headaches, and enhances your mental state. It relaxes your body and acts as a mild sedative, imbuing you with qualities of peace and harmony. Passion flower quiets the mind and the nervous system, leading to deeper contemplation and expanded awareness. Often combined with skullcap in tea, the herb promotes sound sleep and pleasant creative dreams.

RED CLOVER   Trefoil. The body's entire system benefits from this herb because it relaxes you, acting as a tonic for your nerves and a blood purifier. By giving your body a burst of energy and removing negative influences, it purifies the ambient energy inside and around you. In creating sensations of harmony and love, the herb enhances mental perception and awareness, especially clairvoyant abilities. Symbolic of the threefold Goddess and of the trinity, clover was used by Druids to dispel negative energy.

ROSE   A feminine herb associated with water and earth, it is used for magickal power, creating abundance, and divination. Often part of magickal healing and love mixtures, roses have long been placed on sacred altars. The apple of the flower kingdom, associated with health, pure energy, and potential. To better remember your dreams, drink tea of rosebuds before going to bed.

ROSEMARY   Elf leaf. A sun herb, it promotes cell growth and repair, keeping you alert and physically and mentally energized. Bathing in rosemary water makes the old young again, because its curative vibrations are uplifting to emotions and sensations. It is burned as incense to rid a place of negativity and unfriendly energies. Students in ancient Greece wore rosemary twined in their hair to enhance their powers of memory. Burning rosemary on charcoal brings answers to questions and increases personal wisdom.

SAFFRON   A masculine herb associated with the sun, it is used to strengthen magickal ability and assist in merging. Saffron is eaten in honor of the Goddess and is used to purify all healing works. Drinking a saffron infusion gives you prophetic dreams. Used to raise the wind and in love potions.

SAGE   Red sage, sawge. Used as a tonic tea in Spring and Autumn, sage should be used for no longer than a week, up to three times a day. Promoting longevity and strengthening the brain and muscles, the herb is eaten and carried to increase memory and mental abilities. It is used as a headache remedy when combined with rosemary, wood betony, and peppermint. Sage is burned to diffuse negativity before ritual or meditation, and baths with sage purify your entire being. As an herb of Jupiter, it is traditionally eaten in the month of May to promote longevity. Sage vinegar was also used as a protection from the plague. The Jicarilla Apache call sage ghost medicine and use the herb to rid a person of bad dreams and negative influences.

SANDALWOOD   A moon herb associated with water. When combined with lavender, it makes an incense designed to call the Goddess and Gods. It is used for protection and purification, and promotes spiritual awareness. Excellent incense base. Used on the third eye and in a paste for tantra and sex magick. The wood is burned in ritual fires.

SKULLCAP   Hoodwort. One of the best nerve tonics, it soothes and reduces disorders of the central nervous system and feeds the nerves, supporting and strengthening them. As a safe and reliable herb, skullcap can be used freely, as it is essentially nontoxic and is excellent for hypertension and restlessness. It promotes harmony and general sensations of peace and love, relaxing your mind so your thoughts are more expansive, helping you to tap into your higher self.

SUNFLOWER   A New World plant and symbol of the sun. Parts used are the flowers and seeds. The flowers were fashioned into crowns by the Aztec priestesses and carried in ritual. The seeds are symbols of fertility and strength.

THYME   Thyme is an herb of the Faery, used for healing and attracting beneficial energies. It is burned prior to magickal works to cleanse the area or used in ritual baths for purification. Helps to move beyond negative past memories. Sacred to Venus, this herb is used to strengthen magickal power and awareness.

VALERIAN ROOT   Garden heliotrope. Considered an all-heal, the herb is a nerve tonic and promotes sleep. It imparts healing effects on the nervous system, expands awareness, and neutralizes negativity. Traditionally used to raise and commune with the spirit world, valerian helps you connect with various realms of existence. Cats love the smell of this herb. The Romans used it as incense. From the Latin *valere,* meaning "to be strong." It is an herb of Mercury. (Valerian root should not be boiled, since boiling will dissipate the essential oils that contain the therapeutic qualities.)

VERVAIN   Enchanter's herb, herb of grace. Magickal herb associated with Venus, the Goddess of Love. Used to purify the altar and sacred space. Traditionally harvested just before flowering on a dark moon at the time of the rising of Sirius. Worn for protection and dreaming. Vervain is worn during initiation and sprinkled throughout your ritual area and home. Burn this herb to rid yourself of the pain and frustration of unrequited love.

WILD YAM ROOT   Relaxing and soothing and used as a female tonic to balance hormones and sexual energy.

YOHIMBE   Extract from the bark of the mature African coryanthe yohimbe tree that acts as a natural aphrodisiac for women and men. Effective sexual remedy and stimulant.

Appendix D

LOVE, SEX, AND MAGICK CRYSTALS AND GEMSTONES

Crystals are gifts of nature, gifts revered and used by the ancient Chinese, Egyptians, Sumerians, Native Americans, and Celts, among others. According to modern science, quartz crystals and gemstones consist of naturally balanced, solid state energy fields. These energetic field properties can be harnessed for spiritual and magickal purposes.

Quartz crystals and gemstones have extremely high and exact rates of vibration that can be precisely manipulated to augment, transform, transduce, store, and focus other rates of vibrations. By using crystals and gemstones, thoughts can be amplified and transformed, increasing magickal abilities and powers of intention and visualization.

AGATE, BLOOD AGATE, RED AGATE, GREEN AGATE, BANDED AGATE, BROWN AGATE, WHITE AGATE, MOSS AGATE, BLUE LACE AGATE, BLACK AGATE

Magickal Uses: A chalcedony of microscopic quartz crystals for body, mind, and spirit balancing, grounding, building patterns and self-confidence, longevity, protection, self-honesty, scrying, and circulation of sexual energy.

AMAZONITE, AMAZONSTONE

Magickal Uses: Feldspar for luck, prosperity, successful completion of rituals and patterns, growth, creativity, psychic ability, and receiving energy.

AMBER

Magickal Uses: A tree sap called the Wet Jewel. Activates the creative fire within; good for grounding and centering, healing, and harmonizing female and male energy.

AMETHYST

Magickal Uses: Development of magickal skill, spiritual connection, mental clarity, love, divination, wisdom, courage, psychic growth, dreaming, protection, invulnerability, healing, and balancing energy. Increases hormone production, good for circulation of energies, calming nerves, astral travel, doubling out, and second sight.

AQUAMARINE

Magickal Uses: Type of beryl used for clarity in love, sex, and magick. Increases perception; helps to get rid of old patterns and conditioning. Encourages flow, inspiration, peace of mind, and multidimensional experience. Good for protection, courage, centering, clearing negativity, calming energy, and sharpening intuition and psychic abilities.

AVENTURINE

Magickal Uses: The adventure stone, used for healing, sexual wellbeing, activating and expanding your imagination, enhancing creativity, and drawing prosperity to you. Carried as a good luck charm and amulet, especially when traveling. Strengthens perception.

AZURITE

Magickal Uses: Called the Jewel of Wisdom, azurite is a copper-based stone, excellent for amplifying and moving magickal and healing energy. Increases mental clarity and control, and it is helpful when meditating.

BERYL, HELIODOR

Magickal Uses: Provides clarity and is helpful in getting rid of outworn personal habits and painful relationships. Ritual stone for insight, reawakening love, facilitating verbal expression such as words of endearment, intensifying lovemaking, and strengthening your body, mind, and spiritual connection.

BLACK TOURMALINE

Magickal Uses: For ancestral communication, accessing the shadow self, rituals in the dark moon phase, clarification, and purification. Strengthens the aura and repels negative energy. Excellent for protection from negative people.

BLOODSTONE

Magickal Uses: Form of quartz used for divination, weather prediction, getting in touch with your heart, building creativity, physical strength, stamina, clarity, courage, and sexual vitality. Helps to keep magickal energy circulating. Healing stone of knowledge and higher wisdom.

CALCITE

Magickal Uses: A healing stone used in magickal baths when placed under the running water. For transformation, magickal clarity, remembering, changing negative energy into positive energy, and enhancing learning. Helpful in visualization, meditation, focusing, and astral projection.

CARNELIAN

Magickal Uses: A chalcedony particularly useful for sex magick, fertility, activating fire energy and kundalini, and building power and motivation. A stone of creativity. For past-life awareness, focusing, purification, prosperity, protection, and strength.

CHRYSOCOLLA

Magickal Uses: For tapping into your inner voice. Creates a channel for sacred communication. Used to build personal confidence and develop musical ability.

CHRYSOPRASE

Magickal Uses: A quartz for personal insight, creativity, fertility, and cultivating the art of invisibility. For magickal rituals such as out-of-body experience, psychonavigation, and shapeshifting.

CITRINE

Magickal Uses: Enhances mental quickness and clarity. Dispels negativity and is used for personal empowerment. Beneficial for manifesting and magickal patterning.

CLEAR QUARTZ, ROCK QUARTZ

Magickal Uses: All-around excellent magickal stones. Used for dreaming, shamanic journeying, doubling out, balancing energy, clarity, divine communication, higher consciousness, spiritual enlightenment, meditation, and releasing and unblocking energy.

DIAMOND

Magickal Uses: The hardest substance of nature, used for magickal power, good fortune, sexuality, love, inspiration, protection, personal empowerment, and perfecting patterns. The stone is an energy catalyst and amplifies the energy and state of mind of the wearer, be it positive or negative.

EMERALD

Magickal Uses: Beryl used for divination, psychic development, enhancing sexuality, healing, creativity, cleansing, and balancing the body, mind, and spirit, meditation, gaining wisdom, and attaining higher states of consciousness.

FLUORITE

Magickal Uses: For harmony, balance, healing, empowering female energy, otherworld experience, sexuality, spiritual awakening, and out-of-body experience.

GARNET, ALMANDINE, PYROPE, RHODOLITE

Magickal Uses: A stone of passion, love, compassion, friendship, imagination, prosperity, and creativity. Circulates energy and is excellent for love and sex magick. Useful for past-life and future-life experiences, good fortune, and sharpening your perceptions.

HEMATITE

Magickal Uses: Iron oxide used for centering, grounding, and manifesting light and energy. A stone of protection, strength, astral projection, and dreaming.

HERKIMER DIAMOND

Magickal Uses: Clear crystals used primarily for dreaming, experiencing higher love, personal empowerment, and stimulating your psychic centers. The stone filters negativity and is used in past-life experience.

JADE, JADEITE, NEPHRITE, SERPENTINE

Magickal Uses: Called the concentrated essence of love. Used for divine love, learning to receive and give love, meditation, dreaming, and expanded spiritual awareness. Jade is particularly good for protection and ridding yourself of negativity.

JASPER

Magickal Uses: Type of chalcedony used for gem essences, magickal fortitude, prayer, protection, quick thinking, and neutralizing negative influences. Good for grounding and centering.

KUNZITE

Magickal Uses: Heart stone (with lithium) used for receiving love and joy, and releasing painful memories and relationships. Balances your mental and emotional bodies and circulates energy and desire in magick.

LAPIS LAZULI

Magickal Uses: For psychic development, protection, divine wisdom, shapeshifting, and magickal power. Excellent for divination, protection, shielding, self-discovery, and personal empowerment. The stone amplifies magickal energy, expands awareness, and is used in amulets and ritual jewelry.

LEPIDOLITE

Magickal Uses: The lithium content in the stone is helpful for expanding psychic awareness, facilitating out-of-body experience, and increasing awareness. Creates a sense of peace and tranquility, diffuses negativity, and promotes pleasant dreams.

MALACHITE

Magickal Uses: Popular stone for magick. Used for divine communication and communication with nature, promoting visions, and connecting with the animal kingdom. A shapeshifting and prosperity stone used for dreaming, astral travel, and balancing sexual energies.

MOLDAVITE

Magickal Uses: Stimulates psychic ability and intuition, helps in spiritual development, and is excellent when used as markers in the four corners of your sacred circle. Stone of mystical metamorphosis, protection, personal attunement, and shapeshifting.

MOONSTONE

Magickal Uses: Stone of good luck, fruitfulness, true love, intuition, clairvoyance, and healing. Used for multidimensional awareness, divination, creative inspiration, and enhancing desire. Increases sensitivity and sensuousness, and expands your awareness of tidal flows and natural cycles.

OBSIDIAN, SNOWFLAKE OBSIDIAN, APACHE TEAR
Magickal Uses: Volcanic stone used for sharpening inner and outer vision, popular in ritual and ceremony. Excellent for divination, ritual tools such as magick mirrors and altar stones, past-life regression, and getting in touch with your shadow self.

ONYX
Magickal Uses: Used for communication with underworld beings and nature spirits such as devas and faeries. A stone for calming emotions, strengthening your magickal power, building patterns, and magickal confidence.

OPAL, FIRE OPAL, STAR OPAL
Magickal Uses: An eye stone made up of as much as 30 percent water. Used for tapping into cosmic energy, divine inspiration, intensifying emotional states, protection, and gaining wisdom. Excellent for lucid dreaming, doubling out, and harmonizing magickal energies.

PERIDOT
Magickal Uses: For clairvoyance, personal empowerment, balancing energy, promoting vision, and clarity of purpose, enlightenment, and insight.

ROSE QUARTZ
Magickal Uses: For balancing emotions and feelings in friendships and relationships. A love stone used for healing, personal attunement, compassion, and finding higher love. Used for spiritual awakening, restoring faith, fertility, and tapping into your inner voice. Excellent altar stone for love and sex magick.

RUBY
Magickal Uses: For magickal power, personal empowerment, and building magickal energy. A passionate love stone for clarity, enhancing sexuality, activating the life force, and circulating magickal energy. Amplifies energy; used for doubling out, friendship, and meditating on matters of the heart.

RUTILATED QUARTZ, VENUS HAIR, FLECHES D'AMOUR
Magickal Uses: Excellent for directing and storing energy, creating positive energy, strengthening magickal patterns, and healing. Enhances sexuality and physical prowess.

SAPPHIRE, STAR SAPPHIRE

Magickal Uses: For psychic development, diffusing negativity, and developing psychic ability, clairvoyance, and insight. Dispels fear; good for divination, doubling out, astral projection, and balancing body, mind, and spirit. Helps magickal focus and calms emotions. A stone of good luck and healing.

SMITHSONITE

Magickal Uses: For sacred sex, sex magick, strengthening relationships, finding romance, and enhancing emotions and feelings. A healing stone of unity used for developing intuition and multidimensional awareness.

SMOKY QUARTZ

Magickal Uses: For centering and grounding physical energy, and grounding relationships. Diffuses negative energy, balances magickal energies, and is used for crystal gazing and scrying. Makes a good altar stone positioned in the North quadrant.

SODALITE

Magickal Uses: For developing clairvoyance, dreaming, protection, removing energy blockages in the physical body, and mental clarity. Enhances vision and energizes your body, mind, and spirit.

SUGILITE

Magickal Uses: Excellent for dreaming, multidimensional awareness, astral travel, developing channeling ability, and divine communication. Helps to access psychic abilities and charge your energy body.

TANZANITE

Magickal Uses: Used for divination, channeling, out-of-body travel, and divine communication. Helps to expand psychic abilities, gain insight, and develop magickal skill.

TIGER'S-EYE, CAT'S-EYE

Magickal Uses: Stone of invisibility. Used for insight, building magickal patterns, magickal focus, concentration, and shapeshifting. Good for accessing inner wisdom.

TOPAZ

Magickal Uses: For creative inspiration, balancing energies, finding higher love, and building friendships and loyalty in relationships. A stone of healing and knowledge that is excellent in gem essences and recharging physical energies.

TOURMALINE, WATERMELON TOURMALINE, RAINBOW TOURMALINE

Magickal Uses: For magickal creativity and growth, inner peace, harmony, and charging your body, mind, and spirit with energy. Good for polarity work, self-empowerment, spiritual awakening, regeneration, and healing.

TURQUOISE

Magickal Uses: A ritual and ceremonial stone for communicating with the elements, devas, and ancestors, and gaining knowledge and personal empowerment. Excellent for astral travel and sky-walking. A healing stone popular in shamanic traditions.

ZIRCON

Magickal Uses: Looks like diamond and is used for balancing body, mind, and spirit, working with polarities in relationships, and teaching reserve and tolerance.

APPENDIX E

LOVE AND SEX SPELLS AND CHARMS

Never do a work of magick that could potentially harm yourself or others.

Picture Spells and Charms

Use the picture of your lover on your altar and design a love or sex magick ritual to strengthen your love and relationship. The more current the picture, the stronger the spell or charm. Place the picture in front of a white candle for spiritual love or a red candle for passionate love. Rub love oil on the edges of the picture and then create a simple spell, for example, "As the flame of this candle burns completely, the bond between me and my lover grows stronger and stronger," or, "As this candle burns, it brings my lover to me."

Story Charms

Spend some quiet time together talking and making up stories—faery tales, myths, or bedtime stories. Keep the story simple, and every time you are together mention the story or a part of it. This works best if you create names for your main characters and hone in on the same theme each time. Let your imagination run wild and have fun.

You will find these collaborative efforts evolve into personal myths of a kind, evoking strange and exhilarating experiences—mental, physical, and spiritual.

Word or Phrase Charms and Spells

Modulate your voice in patterned ways (i.e., create a specific rhythm or sing-song quality) whenever you say certain things to your partner, such as, "Good morning," "Hello there, gorgeous," "I love you," or "And how are you today?" Use the tone and timing of your words to create a tonality to your relationship, either for a few minutes or for several days. Be careful not to overuse the tone or phrase, or your mate will become aware of what you are doing. At this point, the strength of the voice charm or spell will often diminish. At other times, when your partner starts to realize you are using "the voice," he or she will be flattered and curious as to your attention and effort to get his or her affection.

Whenever you speak with your mate or prospective mate, use a special greeting phrase or saying that is always the same. For example, nicknames are particularly effective, especially if no one else uses or has used the name. Saying goodbye a certain way on the telephone is quite effective: "I will talk with you soon," or "I really enjoyed talking with you, as always." Saying good night in a personal way, such as, "I love you, have sweet dreams," or "Have beautiful dreams, honey," can act as a signature phrase that will trigger a response in your partner.

String Magick and Spellwork

Like the ring, the knot acts as a spiritual bond. By tying three knots in your scarf or a piece of string, you will gain the love of a prospective mate or strengthen the love of your present lover. String magic is a method for harnessing energy. For example, you can learn to control the wind by tying it up. Old wisewomen practiced the art of tying up the wind in three knots. Seafaring people would buy the wind from these women in the shape of knotted rope, scarves, hand-kerchiefs, cord, or thread. When they untied a knot, the wind would blow their sails and move them on their journey. In fact, fishermen's nets are forms of original string magick.

When practicing any magickal work, first choose a location where you can completely focus on your string magick spellwork. Cut two yard-long lengths of string, sit back for a few moments, and get a clear and strong image of what you would like to tie into your life. Remember to thoroughly clear and calm your mind. You should have a positive intention and a clear expectation of what you want. Be aware of the number of knots you make and their numerological significance.

Start by tying the ends of your string together in a firm knot, and then loop and slide the thread in and out of your fingers. Use both hands to cradle the thread as you slide its length in and out of your fingers and knot it. Allow your hands to weave the thread in deliberate and stylized shapes, as if sculpting a face in clay. Turn your mind completely to what you want, what you truly desire. Your fingers, hands, and the thread tell the story of what you want and form a link with the energy of your expectation. Become totally absorbed in your task as you merge with the boundless. The movement of the thread and your hands and fingers become one with your intention, expectation, and desire. Everything becomes connected and joined in light. Weave the energy together.

After you have finished your work, offer the thread to the fire and thank the Goddess and God for their gift. Next time you work the thread, to enhance the effect, try adding humming or whistling a special melody. If you make a mistake, use slipknot magick to untie it or delete it. Just take the same size thread, and instead of tieing the ends together, make a slipknot in the middle. Then take an end in each hand and pull, but don't pull the knot out yet. Fully engage your mind with the energy of what you want to be rid of and transfer this energy completely to the slipknot. Finally, pull the knot out firmly, with the knowledge that untying the knot represents the deletion of the unwanted energy. Burn the string and thank deity.

Symbol Love Magick

Use two paper hearts as a symbol of your love, tied together with red or pink string. Carry these as a charm, talisman, emblem, or other token of your love. This attracts corresponding energy and keeps the power of your magick close to you. For best results, keep it on the right side of your body or near your heart, or put the token where it will be seen regularly, like on the mirror or dash of your car, refrigerator door, or bulletin board.

Tarot Love and Sex Magick

Take out any deck of tarot cards and go through them slowly, one at a time. Pick out three cards that most represent the qualities you desire in your sex life. Place these cards on your personal altar where you can see them clearly. Use three red candles and put the tarot cards in front of them. Carve the names of you and your lover three times on each of the candles, and then rub them with vanilla or rose oil.

Set up your altar with incense and altar tools, and select a sponsor Goddess and God for the magickal work. Take off your clothing and anoint your body, starting at your feet and working upward. While you are anointing your body, chant to your sponsor Goddess or God, saying, "Oh self of selves, arise, awaken, attend unto me." Repeat this at least nine times. Visualize and sense the divine qualities of the Goddess and God filling you. Focus on the tarot cards on the altar and concentrate on bringing the cards' energies and qualities into your sex life. Complete your ritual with solo or couple sex magick. Pull up your sacred circle when you are done, but leave the tarot cards on your altar for three to nine days. The Shapeshifter Tarot cards (please refer to the Source Directory) were designed especially with this type of magickal application in mind.

Crystal Love Spell

The purpose of this spell is to deepen your bond with your lover or draw a prospective lover to you. Cast this spell at night on the new moon, preferably in the springtime and on a Friday.

Draw a sacred circle. Place two pink candles in silver-colored or glass holders on your altar, side by side about four inches apart. Light the candles. Next, place a large clear quartz crystal point between the candles, with the point toward you. Gaze at the crystal and sense or see the image of your lover (or prospective lover) within the center of the crystal. As you do this, chant these words of power three times:

> *Candle light, lover's light,*
> *Burn strong, burn bright.*
> *Crystal fire, lover's fire,*
> *Burn long, burn bright.*
> *Sacred lover, sacred light,*
> *Beloved one, be mine tonight.*

Allow the candles to burn all the way down. Thank the powers that be and close the circle.

Candle Love Spell

The purpose of this spell is to draw your lover to you or attract someone you know and would like to know much better. It is best done on a full moon on a Friday or Tuesday night, considered the nights of love and passion.

Burn attraction incense (please refer to Appendix G: Love, Sex, and Magick Incense Formulas). Set your altar using a white altar cloth, fresh flowers such as roses, and two pieces of rose quartz (rose quartz hearts if possible). Use one central candle (pink, white, or red), in a silver-colored candleholder. Place a photo of the person in front of the candle.

Dress the candle using rose oil and then carve the name or initials of the person you desire to be your lover on the candle three times. Also carve your name or initials on the candle three times, inter-twining your name with your prospective lover's name. Bathe a silver needle or pin in the incense smoke for a few moments. Next, take the silver needle or pin and pierce the wick of the unlit candle. Light the candle and chant three times:

> *Sacred flame, sacred fire*
> *Bring to me my heart's desire.*
> *Sacred light, sacred sight*
> *Bring to me my soul's delight.*

Allow the candle to burn all the way down. Take the silver needle or pin and fasten it to the right top corner of the photo of your prospective lover. Place the photo and pin under or close to your bed. Pull up the circle.

Lover Attraction Spell

The purpose of this spell is to draw your lover to you. You will need a fairly large incense burner with a charcoal block. Use three dried bay leaves, crushing them one at a time between your fingers and placing them, one at a time, on the ignited charcoal. Each time you do this, focus on your lover's image in your mind and say outloud:

> *As these leaves burn in the fire,*
> *Bring to me my heart's desire.*
> *Earth, moon, stars, and sun,*
> *So I say, the spell is done.*

Repeat this chant a total of three times, each time allowing the leaves to burn down. You can also do this spell using a fire or campfire.

Linked Hearts Love Spell

The purpose of this spell is to enjoy a satisfying and loving relationship with your lover. Cast this spell on a Tuesday night, on or close to a full moon. You will need a tube of red lipstick or a red felt pen, a pink 8½-by 11-inch piece of paper, and three rosebuds.

Use the lipstick to draw two interlinking hearts on the paper. Draw the hearts with gusto and write your name and your lover's name inside each of the two hearts with the lipstick or red ink. As you do this, visualize and sense yourself enjoying a very loving and satisfying relationship with your mate. Hold the rosebuds between your hands and charge them with loving and passionate energies. Then sprinkle the rosebuds on the paper over the interlinked hearts. As you do this, say outloud:

> *At this hour, on this night,*
> *I seek to find my heart's delight.*
> *I call upon the Ancient Powers.*
> *Link our love with these flowers.*

Wrap the package around the petals, folding it several times and finally sealing it with red or pink wax (preferably beeswax). Keep this package in your dresser drawer.

Dream Lover Spell

The purpose of this spell is to determine whether the one you love will marry you. Cast this spell on a Tuesday or Friday on a new moon. Use five red rose petals.

In the morning, take the rose petals and put them together in a small pouch or sock. Put them in your left-hand pocket or your purse and carry them with you during the day. At night, before you go to sleep, take the petals from your pocket or purse and put them under your pillow or mattress. You will surely marry your love if you dream of him or her.

Love Poppets Spell

The purpose of this spell is to bond two lovers together. Burn Lover's Incense or Love Magick Incense (from the list of incense formulas in Appendix G). Set your altar up and draw a sacred circle. Light three candles on your altar: green, red, and white. Construct your poppets from two pieces of cloth each. While working on your poppets, be sure to focus on who the poppets represent—yourself and your lover. Before stuffing the poppets, use felt pens to draw facial features and any distinguishing characteristics of yourself and your lover directly onto the cloth fronts of the poppets. Write your names on them. You can also use embroidery or fabric paint as ways to personalize your poppets. To further personalize them, runes or astrological symbols can be drawn or painted on your poppets.

Stitch the poppet figure all the way up, leaving just the top open for herbs. Use herbs associated with Venus, such as damiana, rosebuds, lavender, yarrow, valerian, vervain, or verbena to stuff the poppets. After stuffing the herbs into the poppets, sew the tops closed.

Take a nine-inch piece of green ribbon or yarn, together with an eight-inch piece of red ribbon or yarn. Braid them together, and then tie the braided yarn securely around the two poppets. As you do so, chant this couplet nine times:

> *Two as one, one as two,*
> *you with me, me with you.*

The concept of this spell is that what affects the poppets, the lovers also experience. When you are finished, pull up the circle and put the poppets in your bedroom, preferably next to or on your bed, where you can see them daily.

Love Mojo Bags

1. Put dried red rosebuds, thirteen coriander seeds, and a picture of yourself and your lover into a small red cloth bag or red sock. Then place the bag under the mattress of your bed to intensity your love, passion, and sex magick experiences.
2. To dream of you lover, put equal parts of mugwort, rose petals, lavender flowers, and a small amethyst into a small white cloth bag or sock, and place it under your pillow at night.
3. For good luck in love and romance, place clover leaves, a tumbled moonstone, and three hairs from your head and three hairs from your lover's head into a small green cloth or flannel bag, and place the bag under your bed.

Golden Keys Love Spell

The purpose of this spell is to strengthen and protect your primary love relationship. You can do this solo or together with your mate. Use gold-colored keys on a silver chain. The keys must not fit any locks in your possession. Set up your altar using two golden candles, and draw a sacred circle. Burn the Altar Incense (listed in Appendix G: Love, Sex, and Magick Incense Formulas).

Light the candles, then take the keys and bathe them in the incense smoke, one at a time. Place them back down on the altar between the two golden candles. Hold one key up at a time. Place love energies into the first key using intention, visualization, and by merging with loving images of your mate. Place healing energies and feelings of well-being in the second key, and energies of abundance, prosperity, and wealth into the third key. Mark the keys with symbols that represent love, health, and abundance.

Tap each key, one at a time, with your ritual wand and chant this couplet out loud three times:

> *Keys of love, keys of wealth,*
> *Bring us happiness and good health.*

Allow the candles to burn down completely, and then pull up your circle. The keys are to be carried with you in your pocket or purse at all times.

Love Trail Sex Magick Spell

The purpose of this spell is to intensify the passion and love between you and your lover during sex magick. The spell is done as a prelude to sex magick and can also be used to initiate sex. You will need five flowers; daisies, roses, sunflowers, tulips, carnations, or mums all are good choices.

Before your lover comes home, draw a sacred circle around your home, light your favorite incense, and put on some relaxing music. Next, place one flower on the floor just inside the front door (or whichever door your lover usually uses to enter the house). Somewhere between the front door and the door to the bedroom, drop the next flower in plain sight. Next, place a flower on the floor at the threshold of the door to your bedroom, and then a flower on the floor between your bedroom door and the bed. The idea is to create a love trail of flowers, inviting your lover into the bedroom. Finally, place the last flower on the bed.

Each time you place a flower on the floor, chant out loud:

> *Sacred flower, lead my true love to me.*
> *One flower to bring him.*
> *One flower to greet him.*
> *One flower to guide him.*
> *One flower to meet him.*
> *One flower, heart to heart.*
> *Forever one, no more apart.*
> *So mote it be!*

Allow your lover to follow the trail of flowers to the bedroom. Ideally, you will be on the bed, perhaps dressed in flowers or skyclad. Enjoy your love and sex magick. When you are finished, be sure to pull up the circle.

Lucky Coin Love Spell

The purpose of this spell is to strengthen and solidify the union between you and your mate by using a lucky coin. Set up your altar on the night of a full moon and draw a sacred circle. If possible, use a silver altar cloth, silver-colored candlesticks, and two silver candles. Burn Love Magick Incense (the formula is listed in Appendix G: Love, Sex, and Magick Incense Formulas). Use a silver dollar, preferably one dated with your year of birth. Light the candles on your altar and call upon your favorite Goddess, such as Kerridwen, Isis, or Aphrodite, and favorite Gods, such as Lugh, Rama, or Odhin, to offer their blessings and power to your love spell.

Next, bathe the silver dollar in the incense smoke for a few moments. Take a small photo of your lover and tape or glue it to the heads side of the coin. Then take a small photo of yourself and tape it on the tails side of the silver dollar. Place the silver dollar between your hands, stand in front of your altar, and chant out loud three times:

> *Lucky coin of union and love,*
> *Silver Moon shining high above,*
> *Make myself and my lover one,*
> *So say I, this spell is done.*

Allow the candles to burn all the way down, then pull up your circle and put your tools away. Carry the silver dollar with you always, in your pocket or purse as a talisman representing the close bond between you and your mate. I also suggest you place your lucky coin on your altar during rituals to charge it with divine energy and reinforce the love spell.

Breaking a Love Spell

The purpose of this work is to break an existing spell you have cast. You can use a large incense burner for this spell or light a fire in your fireplace. On the first Saturday night after a full moon, or during the waning moon, place a bag or bowl of dried vervain leaves on the ground outside your front door.

Next, set up your altar and draw the sacred circle. Make sure you cut an energetic gate in the circle to your front door so you can go from inside to outside and back again without breaking the circle. If you are doing this spell-breaking ritual outside, build a small safe fire and draw the circle so it includes the fire.

Call in your favorite Goddesses and Gods by speaking their names and asking them for their help and blessings. Burn smudge, a combination of cedar and sage, to rid the area of any negative energies. Light one white candle and place stones such as amethyst, smoky quartz, hematite, or garnet on your altar.

Go through your energetic gate outside your front door and take a handful of the dried vervain herbs. As you take the handful of herbs, loudly shout the name of the person you want to be free of. Turn widdershins (counterclockwise) three times and go back into your home (to the fire if working outside), and cast the dried herbs into the fire. As you cast the handful of vervain herbs, say loudly:

> *On the eve of* [fill in date] *I cast a spell.*
> *Now, the effect I must quell.*
> *May this spell be undone and* [name of person] *be gone.*
> *I ask this by the first light of dawn.*
> [Name of person] *shall never again return.*
> *So mote it be as these leaves burn!*

Do this entire process a total of three times in a row. Allow the white candle to burn down completely, then pull up your circle. Bury the ashes from the fire in the ground, sprinkling them with dried sage.

APPENDIX F

BA-GUA LAYOUTS FOR THE BEDROOM

Lay the Ba-Gua over the rooms of your house to locate areas in your home that can be used to enhance your relationship, marriage, career, health, and creativity. In the basic Ba-Gua layout, the fame side is in the South, the career side in the North. You can either line your Ba-Gua up directionally, or simply line the door of the room up with the career side by overlaying the octagon so that this side is parallel to and inside the front wall of the room. The eight sides are: career, knowledge, family and health, wealth, fame, marriage, children (creativity), and helpful people (mentors). See the diagram on page 184.

Color is important in creating your Ba-Gua for the bedroom. Red is the color of sex, passion, and vitality. If you want to revitalize your sex life, paint your bedroom red or use a red carpet. Place red-colored objects in your marriage corner to energize your relationship. Pink, rose, and peach are the colors of friendship and love. Bright orange is a happy and healing color. Gold and yellow stimulate the mind and promote communication, while green is the color of growth, abundance, and creativity. Blue promotes feelings of peace and also dissipates negative energies. A blue bedroom or meditation room is very relaxing. White repels energy and can be used for protection from unwanted energies, while purple or indigo stimulate your intuition and inner awareness, enhancing spiritual and psychic harmony. Lavender has a softer intensity than purple and is very good

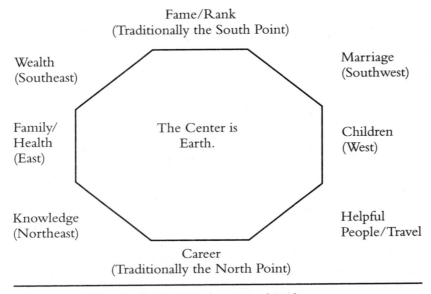

Fame/Rank
(Traditionally the South Point)

Wealth
(Southeast)

Marriage
(Southwest)

Family/
Health
(East)

The Center is
Earth.

Children
(West)

Knowledge
(Northeast)

Helpful
People/Travel

Career
(Traditionally the North Point)

Align the door of the room to this plane.

for meditation and ritual. Black also attracts energy, both positive and negative, and represents the mystery of the unknown. In your bedroom use black sparingly.

Ba-Gua Element and Color Correspondences

(Placing items of these colors in these corners will enhance the corner's energy.)

Marriage: (earth) red, pink, white
Children: (metal) white
Helpful people/travel: (metal) white, black, gray
Career: (water) black
Knowledge/self-cultivation: (earth) black, blue, green
Family/health: (wood) green
Wealth: (wood) blue, purple, red
Fame: (fire) red

Traditional Ba-Gua Power Animals

Place representations of these animals on the appropriate side of the Ba–Gua:

Fame: Associated with birds such as the crane.
Children: Associated with the tiger.
Career: Associated with the tortoise.
Family/health: Associated with the dragon.

Bedroom Ba-Gua Layouts and Cures

(Mix and match elements, using common sense, of course!)

Layout 1: Your bed should always be placed in such a position that you are not surprised or startled by someone entering the bedroom. This particular bed placement is excellent for couples who want to have children or focus their attention on their children.

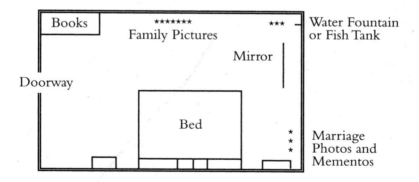

A large mirror is placed directly opposite the doorway on the fame wall to help circulate the chi entering the room. Bookshelves are stationed in the knowledge position, and family pictures along the family/health wall. A water fountain or fish tank (eight goldfish and one black fish) rests in the wealth corner, and marriage photos and mementos grace the marriage corner.

Layout 2: The bed is placed in the family\health position and a crystal ball hangs overhead between the foot of the bed and the doorway. Two large mirrors cure the missing wealth corner, and the dresser with a television rests in the fame area. A mobile (of, for example, birds, the solar system, stars and moons) hangs in the travel corner, and a lamp lights up and warms the marriage corner.

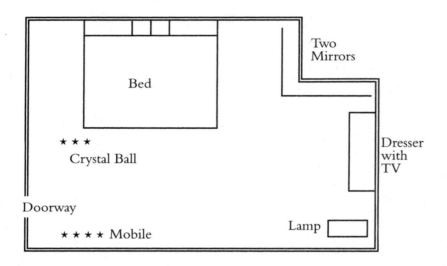

Layout 3: To keep from being pulled away from your successes and fame in life, I suggest you hang a crystal sphere between the door and your feet. Other suggestions would be to place a table of potted plants, or a large statue, trunk, or cedar chest, at the foot of your bed. Two large mirrors are used to cure the sharp, missing, marriage corner of the Ba-Gua. The mirrors are also conveniently positioned by the bed, adding to the visual element of lovemaking. The television is placed in the knowledge corner, and a hanging plant in the wealth corner for growing prosperity.

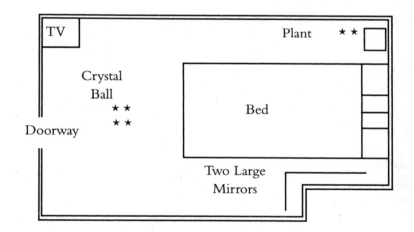

Layout 4: Put plants all along the missing helpful people and children sides of the Ba–Gua, and place a statue or stone obelisk in the marriage corner of the room to solidify and ground your relationship. Put a mirror on the bathroom door, which should be kept closed. This mirror reflects the greenery (growth) from the corner picture window in the wealth corner. In the wealth corner, hang a plant or crystal ball in the window to spread positive chi throughout the bedroom and increase prosperity. The television and computer center are stationed in the career and knowledge positions.

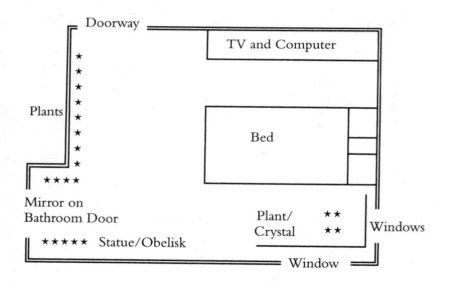

Appendix G

LOVE, SEX, AND MAGICK
INCENSE FORMULAS

Burn the following original incense formulas over charcoal. First light the charcoal disk. These small disks and most of the ingredients in the formulas are available in your kitchen and from health food stores and metaphysical shops. Be careful not to burn your fingers when lighting the charcoal. I suggest using a pair of tweezers to hold the charcoal disk while lighting it. (I also recommend using a lit candle rather than a match or lighter to light it.)

Set the lit disk into the bottom of your incense burner. Use a thin layer of pebbles, sand, or clean soil between the burner and the charcoal block; this will protect the burner. You can use powdered incense formulas prepared beforehand, or you can sprinkle the herbs on a pinch at a time (be careful not to smother the lit disk). Then add drops of oil and small pieces of resin onto the burning herbs. Add the ingredients in the formulas in the order they appear.

Adonis Incense

    1 pinch of red clover
    8 dried red rose petals
    4 dried bay leaves

4 drops of myrrh oil
4 dried red anemone flowers (if obtainable)

Burned to honor Adonis, Greek God of love and fertility. Used to renew love and strengthen love.

Altar Incense

1 pinch cedar
1 pinch cinnamon
6 drops myrrh oil
6 drops frankincense oil or 6 small pieces frankincense resin

Burn on your altar during ritual and magick.

Aphrodite Incense

1 pinch cedar
1 pinch cinnamon
7 drops sandalwood oil
1 pinch marjoram
7 drops amber oil

Burned to honor Aphrodite, the Greek Goddess of love, beauty, and marriage. Used to petition the energies, gifts, and blessings of the Goddess. For attracting a marriage partner, long-lasting love, and fertility.

Attraction Incense

2 pinches rose petals
3 drops dragon's blood oil
1 pinch rosemary
3 drops patchouli oil
9 drops vanilla oil or 1 vanilla bean

Burn to attract potential lovers.

Crystal and Gemstone Cleansing Incense

1 pinch sage
1 pinch cedar
6 drops sandalwood oil
1 pinch rosemary
1 pinch sea salt

In the smoke, bathe the stones you use in ritual and magick to remove all negative and unwanted energies.

Esbat (Moon) Incense

2 pinches rose petals or rosebuds
8 drops sandalwood oil
1 pinch thyme
8 drops frankincense oil or 8 small pieces frankincense resin
4 drops benzoin oil

Burn to attune to the lunar cycles. Enhances the experience of Drawing Down of the Moon.

Friendship Incense

2 pinches sage
1 pinch rosemary
8 drops lemon oil

Burn to encourage love and continuing fellowship between friends.

God of Love Incense

1 pinch cedar
8 drops pine oil
4 bay leaves
1 pinch sage
4 pieces dried orange peel
4 cloves

Burn to summon sacred masculine love. Use to call in the blessings and qualities of the God of love.

Goddess of Love Incense

    3 pinches lavender flowers
    3 drops amber oil
    1 pinch thyme
    1 pinch blessed thistle
    3 drops lotus oil
    3 rosebuds (red)

Burn to attract feminine love, to stimulate your passions, and strengthen your love relationship. Use to call in the blessings, help, and energies of the Goddess.

Incense for Consecrating Ritual Tools

    1 pinch sage
    9 drops sandalwood oil
    3 drops benzoin oil
    1 pinch lavender

Bathe ritual tools in the smoke.

Incense for Romance

    2 pinches mint leaves
    4 cloves
    4 small pieces dried apple
    9 drops vanilla oil or 1 vanilla bean

Burn to inspire romance and romantic feelings.

Isis and Osiris Incense

    1 pinch cedar
    4 drops myrrh oil
    1 pinch cinnamon
    4 drops frankincense oil or 4 small pieces frankincense resin
    1 pinch rosebuds
    4 drops sandalwood oil

Burn to honor Isis the Mother Goddess and Osiris the Father God, who represent the Egyptian polarities of female and male in magick. Excellent for Full Moon rituals.

Lover's Incense

    1 pinch lavender flowers
    9 drops vanilla oil or 1 vanilla bean
    1 pinch jasmine flowers
    9 drops honeysuckle oil

Burn to attract your lover's affections and to create a loving and sensual mood.

Kernunnos Incense

    1 pinch cedar
    1 pinch juniper berries
    4 bay leaves
    4 drops benzoin oil
    4 drops patchouli oil

Burn to honor the Great Celtic Father God or to gain the wisdom and instincts of the Forest God in love and sex.

Kerridwen Incense

    1 pinch sage
    3 drops dragon's blood oil or 3 pinches dragon's blood powder
    1 pinch mugwort
    3 drops benzoin oil
    1 pinch dandelion root
    3 drops pine oil or 3 pine needles

Burn to honor the Great Celtic Mother Goddess and seek her wisdom and guidance in questions of love and romance.

Kundalini Incense

  1 pinch sage
  3 small pieces copal resin
  7 bay leaves
  4 pieces dried orange peel
  7 drops of sandalwood oil

Burn to activate the kundalini.

Love Magick Incense

  1 pinch rose petals or rosebuds
  8 drops amber oil or 8 small pieces amber resin
  1 pinch jasmine flowers
  1 pinch meadowsweet flowers
  4 drops rose oil

Burn during love magick rituals.

Odhin and Frigga Incense

  1 pinch mugwort
  7 drops amber oil or 7 small pieces of amber resin
  1 pinch damiana
  7 small pieces copal resin
  6 drops frankincense oil or 6 small pieces frankincense resin

Burn to summon the all-seeing Norse God of wisdom, Odhin, and the
love of the Goddess Frigga. Use to heal any discord with your lover
and in divination to foresee your future lover. You can also place amber
oil on the tip of your finger and trace runes on your lover's skin.

Pan Incense

  2 pinches cedar
  3 drops dragon's blood oil
  1/4 pinch saffron

3 drops patchouli oil
1 pinch juniper berries
5 small pieces copal resin

Burn to honor Pan, the God of love, lust, and music, and to summon his energies and qualities. Use to encourage sexual adventures and experimentation.

Passionate Days Incense

1 pinch lavender flowers
3 drops patchouli oil
1 pinch jasmine flowers
6 drops honeysuckle oil
1 pinch vervain

Burn during the day to encourage passion, desire, and love.

Passionate Nights Incense

2 pinches rose petals or rosebuds
6 drops ylang-ylang oil
1 pinch licorice root
1 pinch lavender flowers
9 drops sandalwood oil

Burn at night to inspire love, lust, and increase fertility.

Sabbat Incense

1 pinch rose petals or rosebuds
8 small pieces frankincense resin or 8 drops frankincense oil
1 pinch thyme
4 drops benzoin oil
4 drops sandalwood oil

Burn on the Eight Great Days.

Sex Magick Incense

1 pinch damiana
6 drops ylang-ylang oil
9 drops sandalwood oil
1 pinch lavender flowers
6 drops dragon's blood oil
1 pinch powdered coriander
9 drops amber oil or 9 small pieces of amber resin

Burn during sex magick rituals.

Shiva and Shakti Incense

1 pinch rosemary
7 drops amber oil
4 drops benzoin oil
4 drops sandalwood oil
1 pinch rose petals or rosebuds
7 drops lotus oil
4 small pieces frankincense resin or 4 drops frankincense oil

Burn to encourage sacred sexual union and to call in the energies of the Vedic God and Goddess.

Tantra Incense

1 pinch lavender flowers
6 drops amber oil or 6 small pieces amber resin
9 drops sandalwood oil
1 pinch rose petals or rosebuds
6 drops frankincense oil

Burn during tantra practice.

APPENDIX H

LOVE, SEX, AND MAGICK GODDESSES AND GODS

ABTAGIGI Sumerian Goddess of desire and promiscuity

ADONIS Greek God of beauty and love

AGRAT BAT MAHALAT (IGIRIT) Jewish Goddess of sex

AILINN Celtic Goddess of affection, romance, and love

AKUPERA Hindu Goddess of moonlight

ANADYOMENE Sea-born Greek Goddess of sexuality

ANAT Intense, warlike Assyro-Babylonian Goddess of passion and desire

ANGUS OG Celtic God of love and beauty

ANNA PERENNA Roman Goddess of sexuality and fertility

ANNAPURNA Great Hindu Mother Goddess of abundance; giver of plenty

ANU (DANU) Celtic Mother Goddess of knowledge, healing, and fertility

APHRODITE Greek Goddess of love, pleasure, and beauty

APOLLO Greek God of poetry, creative arts, music, healing, and divination

ARTEMIS Greek moon Goddess

ARTIMPAASA Scythian love Goddess who is associated with the moon

ASTARTE   Assyro-Babylonian Great Mother Goddess, associated with the planet Venus

BAST   Egyptian cat Goddess of fertility, pleasure, dancing, music, and love

BEL/BAAL   Assyro-Babylonian sky God of fertility

BHAGA   Hindu God of marriage, fortune, and prosperity

BLATHNAT   "The Little Flower" and Celtic Goddess of sex

BO FIND   Celtic Goddess of fertility

BOANN   Celtic river Goddess of fertility and inspiration

BRAGI   Norse God of poetry

BRANWEN   Celtic Goddess of love

BRIDGET   Celtic Goddess of wisdom, healing, love, and the hearth; keeper of the sacred flame

CHANDRA   Hindu God of fertility and the moon

CHANGO/SHANGO   Great African love God; drummer, dancer, king

CHERUBIM   Hebrew God/Goddess of sexuality and intercouse

COVENTINA   Celtic fertility Goddess of the well (womb)

CUPID   Roman God of love

DAGDA   Celtic God of abundance, love, pleasure, and plenty

DEAE MATRES (THE MATRES, THE IDISES)   Three Mothers, triple Goddesses of fertility and abundance

DEMETER   Greco-Roman Goddess of fertility, marriage, and prosperity

DIONYSUS   Greco-Roman God of ecstasy, sex, revelry, and pleasure

DWYANE   Celtic God of love

EOSTRE (OSTARA)   Celtic Goddess of Spring and fertility

EPONA   Celtic Goddess of fertility, power, and abundance

ERI OF THE GOLDEN HAIR   Celtic Goddess of love and sexuality

EROS   Greco-Roman God of passionate love

FLORA   Roman Goddess of fertility, sex, promiscuity, and Spring

FORTUNA   Lady Luck, Roman Goddess of love and sexuality

FREY   Norse God of fertility, joy, peace, and happiness

FREYA   Norse Goddess of love, beauty, passion, and fertility

FRIGGA   Norse Goddess of feminine arts, associated with hawks and falcons

FULLA   Norse Goddess of abundance and fruitfulness

GERDA   Norse Goddess of beauty and light

GRACES   Three Greek Goddesses of love, dancing, and gentleness

GUINEVERE   Queen of Camelot, King Arthur's wife, and Lancelot's lover

GWYDION   Celtic God of magick, shapeshifting, and eloquence

HATHOR   Egyptian Goddess of love, Mother of creation, and mistress of everything beautiful

HEKET   Egyptian frog Goddess of childbirth and creation

HELEN   Greek moon Goddess of childbirth, love, and fertility

HERA   Greek Goddess of matrimony

HERTHA   Celtic Goddess of fertility and Spring

HNOSSA   Scandinavian Goddess of sensuality and infatuation

ISHARA   Semitic Goddess of promiscuity

ISHTAR   Babylonia Goddess of love, beauty, and war; Goddess of Venus and the morning star

ISIS   Egyptian Mother Goddess, embodiment of femininity

ISONG   African Goddess of fertility

JEZEBEL   Hebrew Goddess of sacred sex

JUNO   Roman Goddess of matrimony

KAMA (KAMADEVA)   Hindu God of love; "the Seed of Desire"

KERNUNNOS (CERNUNNOS)   Celtic Father God of virility, prowess, and nature

KERRIDWEN (CERRIDWEN)   Celtic Mother Goddess of knowledge and inspiration

KHNUM   Egyptian God of fecundity and creation

KRISHNA   Hindu God of erotic delight and ecstasy

KWAN YIN   Oriental Goddess of compassion and beauty

LADY OF THE LAKE (VIVIANA, NIMUE)   Merlin's lover, Celtic Goddess of sovereignty

LAKSHMI   Hindu Goddess of beauty and good fortune

LALITA   Hindu tantric Goddess; cosmic sex energy

LANCELOT   Celtic Knight of the Round Table, champion, and great lover of Queen Guinevere

LOFN   Scandinavian love Goddess who brings lovers together and smoothes over love's difficulties

LUGH   Celtic Master God, including God of love, sex, and romance

MAEVE   Celtic Goddess of sexuality, fertility, and power

MATH   Celtic God of magick and wisdom

MAYA   Hindu Goddess of creativity

MAYAVATI/RATI   Hindu Goddess of passion

MESKHENET   Egyptian Goddess of childbirth

MIN   Egyptian God of sex, fecundity, and crops

MITRA   Hindu God of friendship

MORGANA   Celtic Goddess of love, war, and fertility

MORGAN LE FEY   Celtic Faerie Queen, sorceress, shapeshifter, and beautiful enchantress

NEPHTHYS   Egyptian Goddess of dreams, divination, and hidden knowledge

NIAMH (NEEVE OF THE GOLDEN HAIR)   Celtic Goddess of love and beauty

ODHIN   Norse Father God of wisdom and inspiration

OMAMAMA   Ancestral Goddess of the Crees of Ontario, Canada; Goddess of beauty, fertility, gentleness, and love

OSHUN   African Goddess of love, pleasure, beauty, and dancing

OSIRIS   Egyptian Father God of civilization and rebirth

PAN   Greco-Roman God of lust, love, play, and pleasure

PARVATI   Hindu Goddess of marital blessing.

PENELOPE   Greek Spring Goddess of fertility and sexuality

PSYCHE   Greco-Roman Goddess of love

RADHA   Hindu Goddess of love and sexuality

ROSEMERTA   Celtic Goddess of fertility, beauty, and love

SELENE   Greco-Roman moon and love Goddess

SERAPHIM   Angels of love, light, and fire

SHAKTI   Great Hindu Mother Goddess; embodies feminine energy

SHEILA NA GIG   Celtic Goddess of sex, birth, passion, and laughter

SHIVA   Hindu God of creation; embodies masculine energy

SJOFNA   Norse Goddess of infatuation

TIAMAT   Great Mother Goddess of Mesopotamia who took the form of a dragon

TLAZOLTEOTL   Peruvian Goddess of love

VAR   Scandinavian love Goddess

VENUS   Roman Goddess of love and sexuality

VOLUPTAS   Roman Goddess of pleasure and sensuality

YARILO   Slavonic God of love

BIBLIOGRAPHY

Anand, Margo. *The Art of Sexual Magic.* Los Angeles, Jeremy P. Tracher, 1995.

Bonwick, James. *Irish Druids and Old Irish Religions.* New York: Dorset, 1986.

Bowes, Susan. *Notions and Potions.* New York: Sterling Publishing Co., 1997.

Bulfinch, Thomas. *Bulfinch's Mythology.* Garden City, N.Y.: Garden City Publishing Co., 1938.

Burland, Connie. *North American Indian Mythology.* New York: Peter Bedrick Books, 1985.

Burton, Sir Richard. *The Kama Sutra of Vatsyayana.* New York: E. P. Dutton and Co., 1964.

Campbell, Joseph. *The Masks of God.* 4 vols. New York: Penguin Books, 1977.

_____. *The Power of Myth.* New York: Doubleday, 1988.

_____. *Transformation of Myth Through Time.* New York: Harper and Row, 1990.

Cavendish, Richard. *Legends of the World.* New York: Schocken Books, 1982.

Chopra, Deepak. *Unconditional Life: Mastering the Forces That Shape Personal Reality.* New York: Bantam Books, 1991.

Eliade, Mircea. *Shamanism.* Bollingen Series: Princeton, N.J., 1964.

Feinstein, David, and Stanley Krippner. *Personal Mythology: The Psychology of Your Evolving Self.* London: Jeremy P. Tarcher, 1988.

Ford, Patrick K., transl. *The Mabinogi and Other Medieval Welsh Tales.* Los Angeles: University of California Press, 1977.

Gaster, Theodor, ed. *The New Golden Bough.* New York: New American Library, 1959.

Gimbutas, Marija. *The Goddesses and Gods of Old Europe.* Berkeley, Calif.: University of California Press, 1982.

_____. *The Language of the Goddess.* San Francisco: Harper and Row, 1989.

Goldstein, Nikki. *Essential Energy: A Guide to Aromatherapy and Essential Oils.* New York: Warner Books, 1997.

Graves, Robert. *The White Goddess.* New York: Faber and Faber, 1966.

Gray, John. *Mars and Venus in the Bedroom.* New York: HarperCollins, 1995.

_____. *Men Are From Mars, Women Are From Venus.* New York: Harper-Collins, 1992.

Heath, Maya. *Cerridwen's Handbook of Incense, Oils, and Candles.* San Antonio, Texas: Words of Wizdom International, 1996.

Houston, Jean. *The Passion of Isis and Osiris.* New York: Ballantine Books, 1996.

Johari, Harish. *Chakras: Energy Centers of Transformation.* Rochester, Vt.: Destiny Books, 1987.

Jung, Carl G. *The Archetypes of the Collective Unconscious.* Princeton, N.J.: Princeton University Press, 1990.

Karagulla, Shafica, and Dora Kunz. *The Chakras and the Human Energy Fields.* Wheaton, Ill.: Theosophical Publishing House, 1989.

Knight, Sirona. *Greenfire: Making Love With the Goddess.* St. Paul, Minn.: Llewellyn Publications, 1995.

_____. *Moonflower: Erotic Dreaming with the Goddess.* St. Paul, Minn.: Llewellyn Publications, 1996.

_____. *The Pocket Guide to Celtic Spirituality.* Freedom, Calif.: Crossing Press, 1998.

_____. *The Pocket Guide to Crystals and Gemstones.* Freedom, Calif.: Crossing Press, 1998.

Knight, Sirona, et al. *The Shapeshifter Tarot.* St. Paul, Minn.: Llewellyn Publications, 1998.

Leach, Maria, ed. *Standard Dictionary of Folklore, Mythology, and Legend.* New York: Funk and Wagnalls Co., 1950.

Lin, Jami. *Earth Design: The Added Dimension.* Miami Shores, Fla.: Earth Design Inc., Literary Division, 1995.

Markale, Jean. *Merlin: Priest of Nature.* Rochester, Vt.: Inner Traditions, 1995.

May, Rollo. *The Cry for Myth.* New York: W. W. Norton and Company, 1991.

Millman, Dan. *Everyday Enlightenment.* New York: Warner Books, 1998.

Moore, Thomas. *Soulmates.* New York: HarperCollins, 1994.

Odier, Daniel. *Tantric Quest.* Rochester, Vt.: Inner Traditions, 1996.

O'Donohue, John. *Anam Cara: A Book of Celtic Wisdom.* New York: Harper-Collins, 1997.

Pajeon, Kala, and Ketz Pajeon. *The Candle Magick Workbook.* Secaucus, N.J.: Citadel Press, 1991.

Quan Yin, Amorah. *The Pleiadian Tantric Workbook.* Santa Fe, N.M.: Bear and Company, 1997.

Redfield, James, and Carol Adrienne. *The Celestine Prophecy: An Experiential Guide.* New York: Time Warner Co., 1995.

Sanders, Tao Tao Liu. *Dragons, Gods and Spirits From Chinese Mythology.* New York: Schocken Books, 1980.

Smith, Sir William. *Smaller Classical Dictionary.* New York: E. P. Dutton, 1958.

Stewart, R. J. *Celtic Gods, Celtic Goddesses.* New York: Sterling Publishing Co., 1990.

Telesco, Patricia. *Spinning Spells, Weaving Wonders.* Freedom, Calif.: Crossing Press, 1996.

————. *Wishing Well.* Freedom, Calif.: Crossing Press, 1997.

Tierra, Michael. *The Way of Herbs.* Santa Cruz, Calif.: Unity Press, 1980.

Vogel, Marcel. *The Crystal Workbook.* San Jose, Calif.: PRI Institute, 1986.

Williams, David, and Kate West. *Born in Albion: The ReBirth of the Craft.* Runcorn, United Kingdom: Pagan Media Ltd., 1996.

Worwood, Valerie. *The Complete Book of Essential Oils and Aromatherapy.* New York: New World Library, 1995.

INDEX

Altar
    for Handfasting, 104–5
    incense for, 190
    and magick, 79, 80–84
    and sex magick, 110, 117, 121
    and tantra, 61, 62
    for wine ceremony, 110
An Elder's Herbal, 150
Astrological signs, 95
Austen, Jane, 18

Baths, ritual, 63, 94, 117, 122,
    150
Blake, William, 74
Book of Shadows, 98
Breath work
    and altar tools, 83
    and kundalini, 45–46
    and sex magick, 40, 116
    and tantra, 59, 63
Buddhism, Eightfold Path of,
    44–45

Campbell, Joseph, 10
Candles
    and colors, 137–38

and crystals, 138–39
dressing, 138–39
and love spells, 140–41, 175–76
and magick, 83, 87, 92–97,
    137–41
making, 93–94
and sex magick, 28, 96–97,
    116–17, 140
and tantra, 61
Casablanca, 9
Chakras
    and crystals, 49–50
    and kundalini, 35–36, 43–44,
    46–50
    and sex magick, 59, 112–13,
    119–20
Circle, drawing, 82, 84
Clothing, for magick, 90
Colors
    and candles, 137–38
    and emotions, 91–92
    and feng shui, 66, 183–84
    and tantra, 61
Creative visualization, 29. *See
    also* Meditation

About the Author

Sirona Knight is a contributing editor of *Magical Blend* magazine and a contributing writer for *New Age Retailer, Wiccan Times,* and *Aquarius* magazines. She has a master's degree in psychology from California State University and is a certified hypnotherapist. Sirona is an avid animal lover, a tree hugger, vegetarian, and also a Third-Degree Craftmaster and High Priestess of the Celtic Gwyddonic Druid tradition. Sirona teaches, lectures, has an Internet site (www.dcsi.net/~bluesky/), and is a guest of honor at the Real Witches Ball at Salem West in Columbus, Ohio. She lives in the Sierra foothills of California with her husband Michael, their son Skylor, two beagles, a german shepherd, a chocolate lab, and a family of siamese cats.